100 Years of

Political

Campaign

Collectibles

Mark Warda

GALT PRESS
Distributed by:
SPHINX PUBLISHING
Sphinx International, Inc.
Post Office Box 25
Clearwater, FL 34617
Tel: (813) 587-0999
Fax: (813) 586-5088

First Edition, 1996

ISBN 1-888699-00-0
Library of Congress Catalog Number 96-75315

Manufactured in the United States of America.

Published by Galt Press, distributed by Sphinx Publishing, a division of Sphinx International, Inc., Post Office Box 25, Clearwater, Florida 34617-0025. This publication is available by mail for $16.95 plus $3.00 shipping plus Florida sales tax if applicable. For credit card orders call 1-800-226-5291.

Dedication

To my parents, James and Jennie Warda, who kept politics interesting by nearly always taking opposite sides of an issue.

To the late Professor Milton Rakove of the University of Illinois, who taught me many of my political science classes and who advised me that a law degree would be more useful than an advanced degree in political science.

To Mayor Richard J. Daley's Chicago political machine, which taught me the reality that the best candidate doesn't always win, the best organized one does.

To Richard M. Nixon, who taught me that you don't always know a candidate until long after an election is over.

To the next popular and charismatic president our country finds, whoever he or she may be.

Acknowledgments

Special thanks are due to Mark D. Evans who helped with editing and pricing, Kenneth Florey, who helped locate third party nominees, Tom French, who made available many of the black and white photographs, Lois King, who helped locate some of the buttons and stories (and always has a house full of neat items for sale), Ed Mitchell, who shared his expertise on hopefuls, Richard Rott, who helped locate election statistics, Toni Tolputt, who helped locate web sites, all of the members of American Political Items Collectors, who have preserved much of the information contained in this book and John and Susan Genovese, Ute Glaser, Ed Haman, Shannon Harrington, Lindsay McCoy, and Sidra Quezada, who all helped edit and market the book.

Table of Contents

The famous Cox-Roosevelt jugates

An enlarged photo of one version of the Cox-Roosevelt jugate.
The actual button is less than an inch in diameter.

The campaign button picturing James M. Cox and Franklin D. Roosevelt as Democratic candidates for president and vice-president in 1920 is the ultimate political item. Only about 40 to 60 are believed to be in collectors' hands.

There are five designs of Cox-Roosevelt buttons known. Including different sizes and colors there are thirteen possible, so very few exist of any one button.

The reasons there are so few remaining include the fact that the Democratic party did not have a lot of money for buttons in 1920, their candidate was not very popular, the buttons were not especially attractive, so there was little reason to save them.

The reasons this button is so highly sought-after are that most collectors of political buttons would like to get one button for each presidential ticket picturing both candidates (a jugate) and there are many collectors of the political buttons of Franklin Roosevelt. To them his pre-presidential buttons are especially desirable.

For many years the highest price ever paid for any button was $33,000, paid by the late labor lawyer Joe Jacobs, an F.D.R. specialist, who out-bid Steve Forbes for a unique Cox-Roosevelt. Recently, an especially nice example has reached the $50,000 level, though more common versions have sold for much less.

Introduction

Nineteen ninety-six marks the 100th anniversary of the political campaign button as we know it. While earlier elections did see the use of medals and badges, 1896 was the first year that colorful buttons were used to support presidential candidates. And though the manufacturing process may have changed slightly, our political buttons today are very similar to those of a hundred years ago.

By studying the buttons and other campaign items from the last 100 years we can also learn that the issues in the campaigns were not all that different from today, that the concerns of our grandparents were the same as our concerns. Supporters of the Republican nominee, William McKinley, wore buttons in 1896 demanding "Sound Money" and today Republican buttons say "Balance the Budget." Supporters of Franklin Roosevelt in 1932 wanted a social security program. Democrats today want to avoid cutting the benefits of social security recipients.

This book offers a history of political campaign memorabilia from the last 100 years of American presidential campaigns and includes items of all types. It is meant to be useful to the historian, the collector and those who want to learn more about American politics.

While the historian may be offended by putting a price on history, the collector is eager to know what an item will cost him or what an item he discovers is worth. Since this book is about collectibles, there is a need to let the reader know what it will cost to collect an item. To better understand the pricing of political items see, Understanding Pricing and Value, page 166.

The hobby of collecting political campaign items is relatively young. While there were surely people who saved political buttons and trinkets since the first George Washington inauguration, the hobby of collecting political items was not formally organized until 1945 and the first catalogs were not published until the 1960s and '70s. Compare this to stamp and coin catalogs which have been available for well over 100 years.

Collecting political campaign items is not like collecting coins or stamps. Coins and stamps are produced by the government in known quantities. Every variety has been cataloged and values are easy to determine. But political campaign items were produced by hundreds of private companies and local committees. For most items there is no record of how many were made and we will probably never know of all of the designs and varieties. New discoveries are being made every year.

Because of this factor, the hobby has become very addictive for many collectors. The excitement of finding an unknown item at a flea market or getting a $1000 button for $10 at an antique store has many collectors travelling the country, checking every flea market, scouring every possible source for political items.

Terms

Like any hobby, political item collecting has certain terms which make it easier to discuss common objects which are hard to describe.

A **jugate** (pronounced joo-get) is an item which pictures two persons, usually the presidential and vice-presidential nominees. Items picturing senator and governor candidates or a presidential candidate and a lower office candidate would also be jugates.

Similarly, a **trigate** pictures three people, often the presidential, vice-presidential and gubernatorial nominees. And a **quadragate** pictures four people, etc.

A **celluloid** button is one which is made by putting a piece of clear celluloid over a printed button paper, wrapping it around a metal shell and crimping it in the back around a metal collar. Today other materials such as vinyl, mylar and plastic are used but the buttons are still called celluloids, or **cellos**.

A lithographed button, or **litho**, is made by printing the button design directly on a sheet of metal (often called tin, but actually iron). The button is then punched out and then curled on the edges to hold the pin.

A **tab** is a flat piece of lithographed metal which has (naturally enough) a tab at the top which can be folded over to attach the item to a collar, lapel or pocket. Many tab collectors include similar items such as tobacco tags in their collections.

When moisture gets underneath the paper of a celluloid button, either during manufacture or after distribution, it can cause the metal surface touching the paper to rust. This causes stains in the paper called **foxing**. Foxing greatly diminishes the value of a button.

Political collectors have a special word for fake buttons, **brummagem**. This is an old English word meaning a showy but worthless thing.

The American Political Items Collectors, or **APIC**, is the only organization of collectors of political memorabilia. It offers a monthly newspaper, a scholarly magazine three times a year and local, regional and national conventions where political items of all types are bought, sold and traded.

A note regarding photos and prices

The black and white photos in this book are either full size or the reduction percentage is given to the lower left of the photo. The number represents the percentage to which the item has been reduced.

The prices are the author's best estimate of what a collector would need to pay to obtain an item. The amount paid by dealers for these items would be less.

As explained in Part III, political items do not have fixed prices. For this book we have used ranges to indicate the prices at which the items have recently sold.

Part I - History

The History of Political Items

The first American political items were clothing buttons made to commemorate George Washington's inauguration. These have always been popular collectibles, but they were mementos of the event, not campaign items used to determine an election

Washington inauguration clothing button.

In the early days of our nation there were not presidential campaigns as there are today. In those days the electoral college played a much bigger role and voters, who were all white males, were not subject to the type of campaign we know today.

$800-$1200

Most political artifacts from before 1840 are articles made for sitting presidents. In 1840 the campaign of William Henry Harrison (nicknamed "Tippecanoe" because of his success at a battle at that town) grabbed the public's attention and resulted in numerous campaign items being issued. These were mostly tokens, many of which were holed and worn on peoples' jackets.

Large Lincoln ferrotype button.

$3000-$4000

By the time of Abraham Lincoln's election in 1860 photography had been invented and the tokens of the time added metal-plate photographs of the candidates, known as "ferrotypes." Many ferrotypes are known for Lincoln and all of his competitors for the presidency.

A few elections later, the ferrotypes were replaced with less-expensive cardboard photographs and photographic pins in a much greater abundance.

Over the next few elections, political campaign items became more and more interesting, but in 1893 the big break came. In that year the celluloid button was patented. In 1896, the next presidential election year, hundreds of campaign buttons were manufactured in numerous designs. This began the "golden age" of political campaign buttons in which thousands of beautiful and colorful buttons were released. Compared to the past these were relatively inexpensive and extremely popular.

Since then the button has not changed very much. Some elections produced mostly dull and uninspiring buttons. But every election produces some gems and some classics, buttons which capture the issues and feeling of the times.

Moving eyes and spinning arrows were added to buttons by some manufacturers. When batteries became small enough, buttons were able to include flashing lights and music. With inexpensive computer chips perhaps buttons will soon talk.

Other campaign items have appeared and disappeared over the years. Watch fobs were popular when most men carried pocket watches. Umbrellas, fans, glassware, bars of soap, bandanas, pocket knives, clickers, whistles, combs, cigarettes, rainbonnets, pot holders, even condoms have been adapted for use as campaign items to advertise a candidate.

While most of these have been discarded after the election, some have survived. Whether as a memento of a hard-fought campaign, or as a tribute to an admired president, some people have put away their souvenirs for the future.

As we watch our current crop of candidates, we can look at these items and wonder how we would feel if Teddy Roosevelt, FDR, Ike or Kennedy were running today.

Viewing History Through Political Items

A collection of political campaign buttons gives a clear view of the issues of the day, and of the claims and promises made in the campaigns. Nearly every contemporary slogan, from the common to the crude, made its way onto a button.

1896-1900

16 to 1

$30-$40 $500-$700 $30-$40 $2500-$3000

One of the biggest issues in the races between William McKinley and William Jennings Bryan was the issue of silver coinage. Silver interests in the west wanted their silver to be valued at one-sixteenth of an ounce of gold. Thus their slogan was "16 to 1" and their candidate was Bryan, who supported their cause.

Popular Democratic buttons showed a clock with the time being 16 minutes to one, a daisy with 16 petals and one center, or just the numbers "16/1."

Gold bugs and silver bugs

$25-$35 $175-$225 $100-$150 $350-$450

Because the issue of silver coinage was one of the main platforms of the Democratic party, silver became their symbol and their supporters were called silver bugs. Republicans were called gold bugs and their color became gold.

The buttons of the era reflected this issue clearly. Most McKinley buttons used the gold color and most Bryan buttons used silver. Simple gold and silver pins in the shape of beetles and other bugs were made and the wearing of these indicated the position of the wearer.

Some of the gold and silver bugs had a latch on them which, when pressed, allowed the wings to open, showing the photos of the candidates. These were among the most popular political items 30 years ago, and are still popular, but the prices haven't risen much lately.

Free Silver

The proponents of silver wanted the ability to produce silver coins which would circulate freely in the country. Their slogan was "free silver."

$100-$150

Sound Money

Those who opposed the issuance of silver at the ratio of 16 to one claimed that allowing the issuance of unlimited silver coinage would debase the currency and cause inflation. They therefore said that their position was for "sound money," as opposed to unlimited silver coinage and numerous items were issued on the sound money theme.

$75-$125 $30-$40

Full Dinner Pail

$80-$120

$150-$250

The "full dinner pail" was a symbol of the Republican party and appeared on several buttons of the era. The Democratic answer was a dinner pail with the bottom fallen out of it, or the slogan "the empty dinner pail."

Protection and Prosperity

Since the Republican policies of the era included protective tariffs for some American industries, one slogan which was used on buttons, bandannas and other items was "Protection to Home Industries."

$25-$35

$200-$300

Crown of Thorns

Bryan's most famous speech, which is still known as one of the most moving speeches in American history, is his "Cross of Gold" speech in which he implored that a crown of thorns not be pressed "down upon the brow of labor" and that mankind not be crucified "upon a cross of gold." This inspired several buttons and some even painted real thorns gold and attached them to ribbons to be worn as campaign items.

$300-$400

$300-$400

Talked to death

Apparently, the issues of the 1890s captured the interest of the populace and were popular subjects of daily discussion. Some people grew tired of the subjects and produced little coffins with the slogan "talked to death."

$200-$300

1904-1912

After the assassination of President McKinley in 1901, Teddy Roosevelt became both the new president and an American icon. A "Rough Rider" in the Spanish-American war, a big game hunter in Africa, and a rebel who started his own political party when he disagreed with the Republican party, Roosevelt captured the center stage of the era. During the 1912 campaign he was the target of an assassination attempt but went on to give his speech before having the bullet removed.

Teddy Roosevelt

$125-$175

$800-$1200

Teddy Roosevelt brought his own symbols to the presidency. His wire-rimmed "pince-nez" glasses, toothy wide grin and "Rough Rider" image were symbols which were used throughout his campaign and on many buttons and other campaign items.

$200-$250

Teddy Bears

$10-$20

There is some dispute as to how the "Teddy Bear" originated. The most likely story is that it started when President Roosevelt went on a hunting trip in which not many animals were encountered. Finally a bear was sighted, but it was so young that Roosevelt refused to shoot it. When the story circulated political cartoonist Clifton Berryman illustrated the incident for the papers. Morris Michtom, a Brooklyn candy store owner saw it and asked Roosevelt for permission to call the bear dolls his wife made "Teddy Bears." Permission was granted, the toy company took off to become Ideal Toy Company, and the Teddy Bears became ubiquitous.

My Hat is in the Ring

$20-$35

$300-$500

$60-$90

Roosevelt's 1912 statement "my hat is in the ring" inspired a number of campaign items.

Square Deal

The "square deal" became the symbol of Roosevelt's campaign and inspired several campaign items.

$30-$60

Stand Pat

Fear of the unknown has often been used by political candidates who are in office to invoke fear of change. "Stand pat" was a slogan used by Roosevelt's supporters.

$300-$350

Equality

$3000-$5000

A controversial event in President Roosevelt's administration was his dinner with Booker T. Washington in the White House. This was at a time when the races were segregated, and some people were appalled that the president would invite a black man to dinner. Republicans issued buttons picturing this event to gain support in the black community, and some Democrats issued similar buttons to aggravate racists. The Democratic version of the button pictured Washington as bigger and blacker than the Republican button.

Alton Brooks Parker

Poor Alton Brooks Parker, to be chosen to oppose one of the most popular American presidents in history, and to end up the only major presidential candidate about whom a biography has never been published (other than a campaign biography). As a candidate during the "golden age" of political buttons there were numerous designs made for his campaign, yet no unique slogans or clever sayings. "Good bye, Teddy" was about the best they could come up with. The most interesting button issued for parker is the "White Elephant" design which is included with the color photos in this book.

$40-$60

Bill vs. Bill

50% $75-$100

When Teddy Roosevelt declined to run for president in 1908 and selected as his successor William Howard Taft, the election was a contest between "Bill" Taft and "Bill" Bryan who was making an unprecedented third try for the presidency.

Bull Moose

$40-$75 $30-$50 $20-$30 $4000-$5000

After Teddy Roosevelt returned from big game hunting in Africa and found President Taft was not pursuing policies he supported, he attempted to wrest the 1912 Republican nomination from Taft. When this was not successful he formed a new political party, the Progressive or Bull Moose party. The bull moose was chosen as the party's mascot. Some believe it was related to Roosevelt's saying that he felt "fit as a bull moose" but it is also claimed to be named after Roosevelt's friend, Edwin A. Merritt, speaker of the New York Assembly who was known as Bull Moose.

Quit kickin' my dawg

The campaign slogan of William Beauchamp "Champ" Clark, a hopeful for the Democratic nomination for president was "They gotta quit kickin' my dawg aroun.'"

$20-$30 $20-$30

1916

Stand by the President

$10-$15

The third party campaign by a former Republican president was seen to be the only reason a Democrat, Woodrow Wilson, could capture the presidency. When the 1916 election came around, the candidacy of a former Supreme Court Justice, Charles Evans Hughes, was expected to return the presidency to the Republicans. One newspaper even headlined Hughes as the winner of the election (before all votes were in). See page 142. But the Democrats took advantage of American patriotism during the first world war and asked citizens to "Stand By the President."

8 Hour Day

Since the Adamson Act of 1916, limiting railroad workers to an 8 hour workday, was passed during Wilson's first term, this was played up by the Democrats since workers in

$50-75

$4000-$6000

other industries were clamoring for similar laws.

1920-1924

$10-$15

$10-$20

After the golden age of buttons in 1896-1912, political campaign buttons became quite boring. Most buttons were black or brown and there were not very many clever items. The Republicans were clearly in the majority and the Democratic Party did not have much money to spend on buttons. Consequently, the buttons of James Cox and John Davis are some of the scarcest and most valuable of all political buttons of the 20th century. Only about 40 to 60 Cox-Roosevelt jugate buttons are known in the hobby and their value has now reached the $10,000 to $50,000 range.

League of Nations

After the first world war a goal of the Democratic party was to have America join the League of Nations, the precursor of the United Nations formed after World War II.

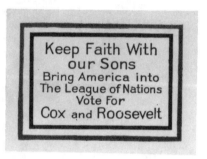

$50-$75

A convict for president

$1000-$1500

In 1920 Eugene V. Debs ran for president while serving time in prison for opposing America's position in World War I. He was the candidate of the Socialist party and received nearly a million votes. His followers considered him a political prisoner.

Teapot Dome Scandal

The most exciting political event of the 1920s was the Teapot Dome scandal, in which members of President Harding's administration were charged with giving oil leases of federal lands to friends. While some say this situation caused Harding's early death, and some of his cabinet members went to jail, the

$400-$500

scandal did not stop Calvin Coolidge from capturing the White House in 1924.

Keep Cool with Coolidge

$45-$85

$20-$25

The main issue of the election of 1924 was the Republican candidate, Calvin Coolidge, and his record since succeeding to the presidency after the death of president Harding. He was known as "Silent Cal" and is still remembered for his statement that "the business of America is business." "Keep cool with Coolidge" was a slogan used on many campaign items of the era.

Another Bryan

After William Jennings Bryan had run and lost on the Democratic ticket a record three times, some thought it was not wise for John Davis, the Democratic presidential nominee to choose Bryan's brother, Charles W. Bryan, to be his running mate. Possibly he thought it was an easy way to pick up the votes of all of Bryan's followers.

$1200-$2400

1928-1932

A Christian in the White House

$20-$25

One issue in the campaign of 1928 was the fact that Al Smith, the Democratic nominee, was a Catholic. No Catholic had ever been elected president and opponents of Smith used this fact as a scare tactic. Because some did not consider a Catholic to be a "Christian," the button at left was issued.

The Great Depression

The Great Depression, which was considered to have begun with the stock market crash in 1929, the first year of President Hoover's term, was the issue of the 1932 election. Both parties claimed to have the answer to bringing back prosperity, but Hoover was at a disadvan-

$90-$120

tage since he had already tried for three years without success. The button pictured has a string attached to the donkey's nose which, when pulled, causes the donkey to rear up and kick the elephant.

Repeal

By 1932, prohibition, the outlawing of alcoholic beverages by constitutional amendment, was considered by many to have been a failure. Not only were the laws ignored by millions of Americans, but a great crime wave overtook the country as mobsters moved in to fill the desires of the public. (Similar to drug prohibition today.)

$20-$35

$3-$5

One promise of the Democratic party in 1932, which helped its re-election, was the repeal of prohibition. Imagine, being able to promise the American electorate the end of a depression and legal beer, too!

A Stamp Collector for President

Franklin Roosevelt's membership in the stamp collectors' organization, the American Philatelic Society, was publicized by his stamp-collecting followers to drum up support among other collectors. The label pictured was available in four different colors and the design was also used on envelopes.

$3-$4

1936-1944

Sunflowers

$200-$250 $25-$35 $2-$4 $2-$4

Because Alf Landon, the Republican nominee for president in 1936, was from Kansas, and the symbol of Kansas was the sunflower, sunflowers sprouted all over the country among Landon supporters. Some were printed on buttons and some were made of felt and attached to the buttons.

The New Deal

Roosevelt's solution to the Great Depression was his series of programs called the New Deal. For many Americans this was a godsend. For others it was an unconstitutional encroachment on their freedoms.

$30-$50

Fireside Chats

One hallmark of Roosevelt's presidency was his habit of giving "fireside chats" over the radio to the nation.

$8-$15

100 Million Buttons

$15-$20

By 1940 many businesses were fed up with the Democratic programs and numerous governmental regulations. Wendell Willkie, a Democrat who voted for Roosevelt in 1932, switched parties and captured the Republican nomination by orchestrating a grassroots campaign. Thousands of Willkie clubs sprang up throughout the country and they distributed millions of buttons.

Apparently printing companies were acutely affected because more Willkie buttons and stamps appeared than for any other election in the past. For example, out of about 600 known campaign stamps issued from 1856 to 1996, nearly 200 supported Willkie!

Commonwealth & Southern

$10-$20

Wendell Willkie was a businessman who had been president of the utility company, Commonwealth & Southern. Roosevelt's supporters preferred that he remain president of that company, rather than of the United States, and issued the button pictured.

The Third Term

$8-$15

$35-$45

$8-$15

$3-$5

$2-$3

FDR's campaign for a third term was unprecedented in American history. Even many Democrats, such as 1928 presidential nominee Al Smith, opposed him. John Nance Garner was dropped from the ticket as vice-president when he sought the presidential nomination himself in 1940. (Imagine being a good vice president for eight years waiting for the presidency and having the president decide to run again.) It was Garner who said "The vice presidency was not worth a pitcher of warm piss." But the last word was changed to "spit" for public consumption.

Joe Lewis wants Willkie

The announcement by heavyweight boxing champion Joe Lewis that he supported Wendell Willkie, the Republican

$300-$500 $250-$450

nominee was a boon to the party. The played this up in black areas to try to convert their traditionally Democratic votes.

Captain Elliott Roosevelt

$6-$12

When President Roosevelt's son, Elliott entered the armed forces he was made a captain, unlike most inductees who entered as privates. This was an easy incident out of which to make an issue and resulted in numerous buttons.

Frances Perkins

The first woman Cabinet Secretary was Frances Perkins who was appointed by President Roosevelt. She served as Secretary of Labor from 1933 to 1945.

$8-$15

Eleanor Roosevelt

$8-$15

$70-$100

First Lady Eleanor Roosevelt was not immune to attacks against her husband's administration.

Life Begins in '40

$20-$40

The popular slogan "life begins at forty" was revised for the 1940 election by those hoping for an end to Roosevelt's administration.

Fourth Term

$20-$30

$8-$15

$12-$20

$6-$12

$8-$15

If people thought a third term was unacceptable, imagine their reaction to Roosevelt's announcement that he would seek a fourth term. He was accused of wanting a dictatorship, a royal family and worse. Some even pre-empted any future plans by sporting buttons with the slogan, "No 5th term either."

Harold Stassen

Harold Stassen was a "boy wonder" who became the youngest governor of the state on Minnesota and was expected to go on to bigger and better things. His attempts to win the White House between 1940 and 1992 caused him to be labeled a perennial candidate.

$3-$7

The Racket Buster

Thomas E. Dewey, the Republican nominee in 1944 had been a New York district attorney known for his successful crime fighting, as well as a popular governor of New York.

$20-$30

1948

The White House Porch

$20-$35

During Truman's first term an elaborate balcony was built on the White House. This opened the opportunity for a clever button.

Truman's Record

> "The Issue Is
> Truman's Record.....
> Nothing Else!"

$5-$10

One of the campaign slogans of 1948 was "The issue is Truman's record, nothing else." This was used by both those who supported him and those who opposed him.

Civil Rights

Truman was known for his support of civil and human rights and this was used by his supporters.

$150-$200 $200-$300

The Won't Do Congress

$40-$65

When the Republicans won a majority in congress in 1946 they refused to pass legislation which Truman supported. It then became known as the "won't do congress."

4 H Club

The acronym of the popular agricultural 4-H club was borrowed by those who felt that Truman should be defeated.

$25-$40 $50-$75

States' Rights

$15-$20 $25-$35

In 1948 the southern states were upset with what they felt was an encroachment by the federal government on their rights and Strom Thurmond ran as the States' Rights Party candidate for president.

Draft Eisenhower

Similar to, but more successful than the 1995 excitement over General Colin Powell's potential candidacy, a movement developed in the late 1940s to draft Eisenhower for president. Eisenhower

$15-$20

had not yet declared his party affiliation so both parties sought him. Supposedly, because the Democrats had been in control for 20 years, he chose to run on the Republican ticket.

1952-1956

I like Ike

$1-$3 $5-$10 $10-$15

Of all the political slogans of the 20th century, "I like Ike" was probably the most catchy. Credit for its origination was given to button makers, but another story said it originated with the Abilene, Kansas (Ike's home town) high school cheer leaders in 1947. It caught on quickly and campaign items of all types appeared with the slogan. It was also translated into several languages, though its effectiveness would not have been as great.

Madly for Adlai

$10-$20 $35-$50 $25-$35

With "I like Ike" blanketing the country, the Democrats needed an answer. "Madly for Adlai" was one slogan they used and "Adlai and Estes are the Bestes'" was another. Neither was as catchy as "I like Ike" so they occasionally answered the slogan with clever responses of their own.

The Man of the Hour

Previous candidates for president used the slogan "the man of the hour," but because Eisenhower's name rhymed, it fit perfectly.

50% $20-$30

Part-Time President

50% $25-$35

Because President Eisenhower often played golf, he was criticized as being a part-time president. This button was issued to answer that criticism.

Don't let this happen to you!

$20-$30

$20-$30

50% $10-$20

At one point in the campaign a photographer got a photo of Adlai Stevenson with his feet up showing a large hole in the sole of his shoe. The Republicans jumped on the opportunity and issued campaign items showing the shoe with the slogan "Don't let this happen to you." The Democrats used it as a sign that Stevenson was an ordinary guy and even issued sterling silver lapel pins of a shoe with a hole in the sole!

Ike and Chris

Prior to the 1956 Republican National Convention, Harold Stassen announced a move to replace Nixon on the ticket with Governor Christian Herter of Massachusetts. The reason Stassen gave was that the ticket would be stronger and would help many more Republican candidates win. Some sus-

$3-$5

pect the real reason may have been that removing Nixon from the ticket would make it easier for Stassen to win the presidential nomination in 1960. But the effort was in vain. Herter nominated Nixon and Stassen was persuaded to second the nomination.

Joe Smith

$20-$30 $3-$5

When the vote was taken to re-nominate Nixon in 1956, one lone delegate refused to make it unanimous. When asked his name he replied "Joe Smith." He was actually Terry Carpenter, a delegate from Nebraska. The Democrats took advantage of this incident by mentioning Joe Smith on some of their buttons.

Truman's Support of Harriman

When former president Truman disclosed in 1956 that he would prefer that New York governor Averell Harriman be nominated for president, Stevenson's supporters issued this button indicating their displeasure.

50% $25-$40

1960

Jack and Dick

$50-$80

$25-$35

$20-$35 $40-$80 $10-$20

After getting used to a president named Ike the supporters of the 1960 nominees wanted to make their candidate sound just as friendly. So Kennedy became Jack and Nixon became Dick. These nicknames were used by both sides, positively and negatively.

Experience Counts

$20-$30 $40-$75 $8-$15

A common theme, the experience of the incumbent party was used by the Republicans in 1960. The fact that Nixon had been vice president under Ike, and Kennedy was just a young senator was played up.

The New Frontier

Kennedy's program, the New Frontier, surprisingly was used on very few campaign buttons. Because of this, those buttons are highly desirable. The John Glenn button pictured is from 1962.

$35-$45 $5-$15

SOB

$8-$12

After Kennedy said that all businessmen were sons of bitches, several buttons and stamps were issued for those proud to be SOBs. The buttons said "Sons of Business Society," "Save our Business" or just "SOB Club."

1964

Let us Continue

With the 1964 election less than a year after the assassination of President Kennedy, one of the best tactics for the Democrats was to play on the sympathies of the public and call for a continuation of the martyred president's programs through re-election of President Johnson.

50% $150-$175

All the Way with LBJ/LBJ for the USA

$1-$3 $1-$3

After the success of the phrase "I like Ike" in the 1950s, the parties always looked for similar ways to promote their candidates. Lyndon Johnson's initials, LBJ were easily used for slogan buttons, and his supporters came out with two catchy ones. But as usual, the slogans were turned around in an attempt to embarrass him. A much sought-after anti-Johnson button reads, "All the way with LBJ but don't go near the YMCA," referring to a sexual scandal involving a member of Johnson's staff. Another reads, "Part of the way with LBJ."

The Great Society

Just as Roosevelt had his New Deal programs and Kennedy had his New Frontier, Lyndon Johnson announced that his programs would be called the Great Society. Of course this was the subject of campaign buttons.

$4-$8

A choice for a change/ A choice not an echo

$4-$8

Because Barry Goldwater's conservative themes had not before been represented by a national candidate, his supporters felt that the electorate finally had a choice. *A Choice Not an Echo* was both a campaign slogan and the title of a book by Phyllis Schlafley.

Goldwater's Extremism

$20-$30   50% $10-$20

Because Goldwater's views were more conservative than many in the Republican party he was considered by some to be an extremist. Rather than try to moderate his views, he said that "extremism in the defense of liberty is no virtue, moderation in the pursuit of justice is no virtue."

In your heart you know he's right

$3-$5

To answer claims that Goldwater's views were more conservative than most Americans, his supporters used the slogan on the button pictured. The Democratic answer to this slogan was "In your guts you know he's nuts." (Ouch!)

AuH_2O

$10-$15

Plastic bubble is filled with water and gold flakes.

$15-$25

The fact that Goldwater's name could be written as a chemical formula and displayed by showing the two components allowed for some interesting buttons. One contained flakes of gold in a bubble of actual water. Another showed a glass filled with gold liquid. A rebus in the form of jewelry included a berry, a gold nugget and a drop of water. A Democratic button incorporated the chemical formula for uric acid and then added "on AuH_2O."

Goldwater's glasses

Because Goldwater's eyeglass frames were so pronounced, they became a symbol of his candidacy. There were both elephant

$8-$12

and donkey pins made wearing heavy black-rimmed glasses, plain little pins of pairs of glasses, and even cardboard glasses which a person could wear.

Bury Barry

Unfortunately for Goldwater, his first name had a negative synonym which was quickly noted by button makers.

BURY BARRY

$4-$8

Johnson-Keating

One of the few buttons ever issued joining a Democrat with a Republican is a button supporting Democrat Lyndon Johnson for president and Republican Kenneth Keating for senator of New York. This was issued by those who felt that Robert Kennedy had no right to represent New York, because he had moved there solely for the purpose of running for the senate.

JOHNSON
1·B
KEATING
2·A

$10-$15

Poor Man's Party

Henry Krajewski was a third-party candidate for president in several elections. He never received more than a few thousand votes, but he left us with some interesting campaign items.

Die-cut paper sticker $8-$15

1968-1972

Nixon's the One

$1-$2 $3-$5

$75-$100 $3-$7

An early slogan for Nixon's 1968 campaign was "Nixon's the One." This was translated into many languages and used on everything from buttons to shopping bags. As usual, it was picked up by his opponents and made into some anti-buttons, both during the campaign and later during the Watergate affair.

HHH

$1-$2

$1-$2

Hubert Horatio Humphrey's unusual initials allowed for a unique logo of his candidacy.

Pharmacists

$5-$10

$25-$35

$5-$10

The fact that Humphrey had been a pharmacist was also noted on buttons.

The Hippy Movement

$3-$8

$7-$15

Both parties tried to capture the spirit of the hippies and yippies of the 1960s, though their success is doubtful.

Flower Power

Eugene McCarthy's challenge to President Johnson and his surprising showing in the 1968 New Hampshire primary is believed to have contributed to Johnson's withdrawal from the race. Though he lost the nomination to party favorite Humphrey, his movement was the beginning of reforms which allowed George McGovern to capture the

$3-$7

nomination in the following election. The symbol for McCarthy's campaign was the light-blue and white flower.

RFK

Although there was much positive sentiment for President Kennedy who had been assassinated just five years earlier, not everyone felt positive about his brother, Robert F. Kennedy. Supporters of Eugene

$10-$20

$7-$15

McCarthy were especially upset that Kennedy decided to run for president only after McCarthy had a strong showing in the New Hampshire primary and proved Johnson could be beaten. The strong sentiments of the time inspired some interesting slogans on both sides of Kennedy's candidacy. The button about expanding the White House refers to the fact that Kennedy had nine children. An even more tasteless version of the same theme read, "Tie Ethel's tubes."

Anti-LBJ

$5-$15

$40-$80

$7-$15

$7-$15

Not since 1940 had so many "anti" buttons been issued opposing a sitting president. Most of these were anti-war buttons, but others were just plain nasty. A button stating "Hang LBJ by the ears" was based on an incident in which he lifted one of his pet beagles by the ears. The statement "That's the ugliest thing I ever saw" was made by Johnson when he saw a new portrait of himself.

Stand up for America

When George Wallace lost the Democratic nomination in 1968 he formed the American Independent Party and chose World War II hero, General Curtis LeMay, as his running mate.

$1-$3

Tweedle Dee and Tweedle Dum

George Wallace's campaign stressed his claim that there was little difference between the Democratic and Republican candidates but that he offered a clear alternative. Thus one slogan used by his supporters called his opponents Tweedle Dee and Tweedle Dum, characters from *Alice in Wonderland*.

$5-$10

Re-elect the President

$1-$2

The fact that many Americans are patriotic and support their president was noted by Nixon's re-election campaign. Some thought that the less they mentioned Nixon and used "the President" the better, so many buttons referred to Nixon only as "The President."

Dike Bomber

Because it was disclosed that our military forces in the Viet-Nam war had bombed dikes, Nixon was considered by some to be responsible and the button pictured was issued.

$5-$10

Four more years

Another slogan supporting Nixon's re-election without actually mentioning his name was "Four more years." One Democratic answer was "four more weeks" and another was "no more years." One group answered with one of the most disturbing political posters ever produced (so far). See page 79.

Now more than ever

$1-$2

One slogan used occasionally by candidates is "Now more than ever." It was adopted by the Nixon campaign in 1972, perhaps playing on George McGovern's reputation as a radical.

KMA

When McGovern was harassed on an airplane by a woman passenger he whispered to her "kiss my ass" but was overheard by the press. This was picked up and displayed proudly, though not blatantly, by his supporters.

70% $8-$15

Eagleton

50% $5-$10

In an unusual move, Thomas Eagleton was removed from the Democratic ticket after the convention because of disclosures of his treatment for depression. Very few buttons were made for McGovern and Eagleton prior to his withdrawal. Most were made as collectors' items shortly thereafter.

1000%

After Eagleton's medical report was made public, but before he withdrew from the ticket, McGovern made the statement that he was "1000% behind Eagleton." This was, of course used against him later in the campaign.

50% $2-$4

Skinny cats

Since "fat cats" were alleged to be supporters of Nixon, McGovern supporters took on the name "skinny cats" and the pictured button became a classic of the campaign.

70% $75-$175

Come Home America

McGovern's main campaign issue was that American troops should be withdrawn from Viet-Nam. Come Home America became one of his slogans.

70% $15-$20

October 9th

On October 9th, 1968 Richard Nixon gave a speech in which he said, "Those who have had

"Those who have had a chance for four years and could not produce peace, should not be given another chance."

Richard Nixon
October 9th, 1968

$2-$3   50% $10-$20

a chance for four years and could not produce peace, should not be given another chance." This statement was used against him on buttons, bumper stickers and posters four years later, when the war was still not over.

Agnew

$12-$20

$3-$8

Spiro Agnew attracted the attention of the press immediately upon his selection as Nixon's running mate in 1968. His criticism of the administration's opponents with such terms as "nattering nabobs of negativism" assured his place in the hearts of the right and the hates of the left. When he later resigned after disclosure of a bribery scandal from his gubernatorial days, he gave button makers even more ammunition.

Watergate

$4-$10

70% $10-$20

$3-$8

$3-$8

The Watergate scandal and President Nixon's resignation provided plenty of fodder for button makers. Hundreds of buttons appeared, many of which were quite clever. The Martha referred to on the button on the previous page is the outspoken Martha Mitchell, wife of Attorney General John Mitchell.

Rocky

$10-$20 $5-$10

New York Governor Nelson Rockefeller was unsuccessful in his bids for the Republican nomination in 1960, 1964 and 1968. But in 1974 when Nixon resigned, Ford assumed the presidency, leaving the vice-presidency again vacant. Rockefeller was appointed to fill the position, making it the first time in history that neither the president nor vice-president had been elected by the people. Several buttons were manufactured to commemorate the event, and many more buttons are available from Rockefeller's previous campaigns.

1976

Gerald Ford was the first American to become president who had not been elected to either the presidency or vice presidency. He was appointed vice president upon the resignation of Spiro Agnew and assumed the presidency upon President Nixon's unprecedented resignation.

At the 1976 Republican convention, President Ford faced a strong challenge from Ronald Reagan but managed to win the nomination of the party.

Ford

50% $15-$25   70% $8-$15 $5-$10

Since the President's name was the same as that of a popular automobile, many clever buttons were possible.

Ford's Vetos

Because President Ford became known for his many vetos of bills passed by the Democratic congress, some people thought that Ford himself should be vetoed in the 1976 election.

$3-$8

WIN

$1-$2 $4-$8

With inflation rising in the mid 1970s, the government knew it had to act. Among other things, the Ford administration started a "Whip Inflation Now" campaign represented by red buttons with the white letters "WIN." These were manufactured by numerous companies in dozens of varieties. Some private businesses added their name to the button for publicity.

Peanuts

| 70% | $12-$20 | 50% | $4-$8 |

| 50% | $15-$20 | 50% | $10-$15 |

Carter's background as a peanut farmer provided great material for campaign items both supporting and opposing his campaign. The peanut became the unofficial (but unappreciated) symbol of his candidacy. The fact that the elephant was the symbol of the Republican party and elephants eat peanuts, allowed for some clever designs. Reportedly, former president Carter hates to autograph peanut memorabilia from his campaign.

Gritz and Fritz

| 70% | $2-$5 | 70% | $10-$20 |

Grits, a popular food in Carter's state of Georgia, and Mondale's nickname provided a clever slogan.

The grin will win

70% $3-$7   70% $7-$12

Carter's toothy smile, like Teddy Roosevelt's became a recognizable symbol of his candidacy, especially when combined with the color green or the peanut. One slogan used was "the grin will win."

Carter's Playboy Interview

When Jimmy Carter gave an exclusive interview to Playboy magazine and admitted he was guilty of "lust in his heart" it caused quite a stir. Both the magazine and private manufacturers issued buttons commemorating the event.

$12-$18

1980-1984

Free the Democratic 20,000,000

50% $3-$10   50% $3-$7

After the 1968 Democratic convention, many people in the party felt that too much control of the delegate selection process was in the hands of the party bosses. Reforms were instituted which allowed more delegates to be chosen in the primaries. One of the rules, rule F(3)(c), required the delegates to vote for the nominee chosen in the primary. In 1980 this rule effectively guaranteed President Carter the nomination. Those in the party who thought Carter should be replaced, especially supporters of Senator Edward Kennedy, sought to have the rule abolished. Some of their buttons would not be known to be political buttons to those who do not know this story.

Chappaquidick

70% $7-$15   50% $15-$30

Senator Kennedy's accident in July, 1969 in which he drove off a bridge and his female passenger drowned was an issue in his campaign for president and probably cost him the chance to gain the nomination.

Reagan's acting career

$3-$7   70% $5-$10

Ronald Reagan's film career provided much ammunition for jokes about his candidacy.

Jellybeans

Reagan's fondness for jellybeans was, of course, not overlooked as a source for button designs.

$3-$5

Divorce

One would need to know that Reagan was once married to actress Jane Wyman to realize the purpose of the button pictured. As the first divorcee to win the presidency, this button probably started a trend.

$3-$6

PATCO

One of President Reagan's first notable acts was his decision to fire the air traffic controllers who went on strike in violation of federal rules. This button was put out by a union unhappy with that act.

**FIRE REAGAN!
NOT PATCO
MEMBERS**

$5-$10

"We begin bombing in five minutes."

At one point during his presidency Reagan attempted to make a joke about bombing the Soviet Union while testing a microphone. This was not considered funny by the Soviets and caused a minor scandal.

$5-$12

Irangate

$3-$7 $3-$7 $3-$7

When word got out that Iran may have been allowed to purchase American arms as part of the deal to release the American hostages, it caused a scandal. The question raised was whether President Reagan knew about this deal or if it was solely the work of his aides.

John Anderson

Illinois congressman John Anderson bolted the Republican party in 1980 to run under the "National Unity Campaign." He and his running mate, Patrick Lucey, received over five million votes, 6.6% of the total cast.

50% $4-$8

Geraldine Ferraro

In 1984 The Democratic party nominated the first woman ever on a national presidential ticket, Geraldine Ferraro, a member of Congress from New York.

70% $3-$7   70% $3-$6

Fritz and Tits

70% $5-$10

Since the Carter-Mondale ticket had been nicknamed Grits and Fritz, at least four button manufacturers thought that reducing the Democratic vice-presidential nominee to her female body parts would be a clever way to ridicule the ticket. One pictured Mondale with Dolly Parton and included the additional slogan "the three biggest boobs in America," to somewhat confuse the point of the joke.

1988

Dan Quayle

$2-$4 $2-$4   50% $2-$5

One of the biggest issues of the 1988 election was whether the Republican nominee was qualified to be vice president. Quayle's ability to stick his foot in his mouth and to mix his words provided fodder for many button designs.

Gary Hart

Unlike 1992, when accusations of adultery against Bill Clinton had no effect on his candidacy, Gary Hart was persuaded to withdraw from the race when charges of promiscuity were leveled against him.

50% $3-$8

Dukakis

70% $2-$3 $25-$50

Michael Dukakis was the Democratic nominee in 1988. While his buttons are not especially popular at this time, the button pictured is highly sought after. It was passed out by his supporters at the American Library Association convention in New Orleans. Since few collectors could obtain one, the price quickly rose to $25.

Where was George?

$2-$4   50% $3-$7

At the Democratic National Convention a popular speech given by Senator Edward M. Kennedy repeated the refrain, "Where was George?" This alluded to the question of what part Bush played in the scandal involving arms being traded for hostages (called Irangate or the Iran-Contra scandal by some). Like most slogans, the opposition was able to turn it around and come up with a good answer. The above answer alluded to the Chappaquidick incident in which Kennedy was neither sober nor with his wife.

Bush

$3-$6 $3-$6   70% $2-$6

Risque political slogans have a special fascination for Americans and George Bush's name provided a clear opportunity for those with warped minds. Some entrepreneurial collectors had a batch of hard candy manufactured with the slogan "Bush in '92" made into each piece. They were packaged in bags which said "Bush on Every Tongue" similar to a 1950s package of candy which urged people to put "Ike on Every Tongue."

1992

Clinton's Saxophone

$3-$5

70% $5-$8   70% $4-$8

An instrument like a saxophone is a perfect symbol for a candidate. It becomes clear to the public that it represents the candidate and it is not easily used in a negative way.

Bus tour

70%   Hand painted wooden pinback $5-$10

$3-$6

After the Democratic convention Clinton and Gore went on a multi-state bus tour to gather support for their campaign. As they stopped along the way, both the party organizations and private vendors used the events for the issuance of special buttons.

Hope

70% $3-$8

The fact that Clinton was born in Hope, Arkansas provided ideas for several button designs.

Sexual proclivities

One of the big issues of the 1992 campaign was the claim that candidate Clinton had engaged in extramarital affairs. This was not a new type of accusation. Over 100 years earlier Grover Cleveland was taunted with the slogan "Ma, ma, where's my pa? Gone to The White House, ha, ha, ha," refering to an accusation he had an illegitimate child.

70% $2-$4

Inhale to the Chief

Clinton's admission that he had smoked marijuana (though it was outside the jurisdiction of the United States and he claimed that he did not actually inhale it) was picked up by his opponents as a campaign issue and by button makers as a gold mine.

70% $2-$3

The draft

As the first president born after World War II, Clinton had to contend with the issue of his lack of military service. The fact that he had actively sought to avoid the draft as a student was raised loudly by the opposition, but to no avail.

70% $2-$3

Socks

70% $2-$3   70% $2-$3   70% $2-$3

Once Clinton was elected the country had a "first cat." Socks became popular with the press on slow news days and with button makers.

Quayle's "Potatoe"

At one of his appearances Vice-President Quayle participated in a spelling bee. When he turned out not to know that potato did not have an "e" in it, he was ridiculed across the nation. As it turned out, he had been given a cue card on which potato was spelled wrong (by a Democrat?) which lead him astray.

70% $5-$10

Brown's 800 Number

70% $3-$8

Jerry Brown was the first candidate to personally promote his 800 phone number wherever he went, and he became widely known for this. The button pictured became popular among Brown opponents and candidate Bill Clinton obtained one for his own button collection after admiring it on the shirt of one of his supporters.

We're Mad as Hell

70% $3-$8

70% $3-$8

The public's frustration with politics as usual lead to the candidacy of Ross Perot as an independent for president. While he did not win any electoral votes, he received a greater percentage of votes than any third party since Teddy Roosevelt bolted his party in 1912. Because most of Perot's support was grass roots, there were hundreds of buttons made by local organizations with no instructions from above. Locating every Perot button issued could take a lifetime.

Whitewater

What did Foster know?
Release the truth now!

70% $3-$6

Gore in '94

70% $3-$6

Foster
Nussbaum
Hubbell
Give it up, Bill

70% $3-$5

Watergate
Iran-Contra
Whitewater
Enough already!
PEROT
in '96!

70% $3-$5

As the Clinton's land deal in the Arkansas Whitewater development came under more careful scrutiny after the election, more questions arose and a special prosecutor was appointed. Some predicted the downfall of Clinton's presidency but as of early 1996 the Clintons survived all attacks.

Hillary Rodham Clinton

70% $2-$3   70% $2-$3

70% $2-$3   70% $2-$3

President Clinton's wife, Hillary Rodham Clinton, is the most controversial First Lady since Eleanor Roosevelt, and perhaps of all time. As a successful lawyer in her own right, she was more of an equal to the president than a "First Lady." Some found this exciting; others, inappropriate.

1996

70% $2-$3   70% $2-$3

As this book goes to press, it appears certain that the nominees of the major parties will be Bill Clinton and Bob Dole. Dole's nomination makes it likely that sunflower buttons will proliferate, as they did in 1936, but other than that, the most clever campaign buttons of 1996 have probably not even been conceived yet.

70% $2-$3   70% $3-$4

70% $2-$3   70% $2-$3

70% $2-$3   70% $3-$4

Franklin D. Roosevelt, 1932, 1936, 1940, 1944. These buttons represent all four of his campaigns for president. Largest buttons are 1-1/4 inch. Top row: $200-$300, $30-$45, $50-$70, $200-$250. Second row: $25-$30, $10-$20, $5-$10, $8-$12.

Alfred M. Landon, 1936. Because Landon was from Kansas and the sunflower is the state flower of Kansas, sunflowers were used on many of his buttons. Largest buttons are 1-1/4 inch. Top row: $30, $50-$75, $15. Second row: $12, $100, $20, $10-$15.

Ronald Reagan, 1968, 1980, 1984. Button in lower right, 1968. Large button is 3-1/2 inch. Top row: $3-$5, $8, $3-$5. Second row: $8-$10, $10-$20, $10-$20.

Jimmy Carter, 1976. Small buttons are 1 inch. Top row: $3-$6, $3. Second row: $1 each.

Bush/Quayle Golf umbrella $35.

6 inch Reagan button $5-$10.

Carter bank $20-$30, Carter wind-up doll $20-$30.

This is a collection of buttons for most of the candidates from the 1968 election. Many collectors try to get at least one button for each candidate in each election. Ideally a collector would like a jugate for each party but for some candidates there were no jugates. These buttons would sell for $3 to $10 each.

Debs/Hanford jugate paperweight, 1904. Only one known. $1500-$2500.

Humphrey/Muskie plastic
hat $3-$6.

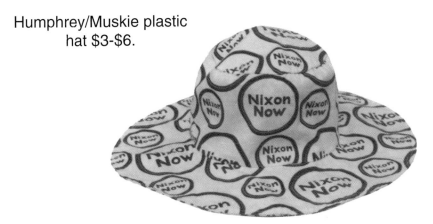

Nixon cloth hat 1972 $20-$25.

Clinton, 1993. Barrel of Clintons satirical game, 1994, $10.

MacArthur, 1940s. Ceramic mug made in occupied Japan, $20-$35.

Perot, 1992. The first button in the bottom row was made from an actual $2 bill. Top row, $5-$10, $4-$8, $5. Bottom row, $10-$15, $3-$5, $4-$10.

Libertarian party presidential campaign buttons 1972, 1976, 1980, 1984, 1988, 1992. Jugates for the Libertarian party have only been available from private vendors. Top row, $20-$40, $3-$5, $5-$10. Bottom row, $4-$8, $3-$5, $3-$6.

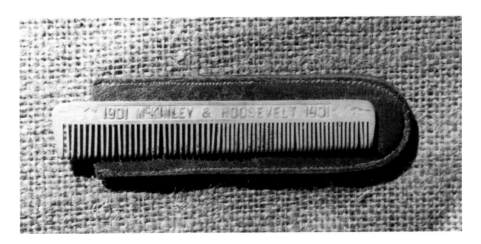

McKinley/Roosevelt aluminum comb, 1901, $100.

Robert F. Kennedy, 1968. Since Kennedy did not live long enough to gain the nomination, he is considered a presidential "hopeful". Top row, $7-$10, $5-$10, $8. Bottom row, $5-$10, $5-$10, $5-$10, $10-$20.

Billary Beer. $2 a can.

Perot cap, $5.

Roosevelt and Willkie, 1940. Matching automobile reflectors. $20-$30 each.

Parker, 1904. The most classic of all Parker buttons. This example has several cracks which lower the value considerably. If mint $400-$500.

Hoover and Smith, 1928. Matching set of rings. $20-$30 each.

Kennedy, 1960s. Halloween mask. $20-$25.

Carter, 1980. Billy Beer and peanuts shirt. $20-$30.

Nixon, 1970s. Halloween mask $20-$25.

Selection of thimbles. Note the switch to plastic. While thimbles are not used as much today as in the 1920s, manufacturers still make them as collectibles for political campaigns. $10-$20, $10-$20, $50-$75, $1-$3.

Selection of 3-1/2 inch buttons. Two are fairly common but three are among the toughest to find. Top row, $25-$35, $250-$350, $150-$175. Bottom row, $5-$10, $100-$130, $3-$6.

Roosevelt and Parker, 1904. A matching set of bandanas. $250 to $350 each.

Kennedy, 1960. Felt pennant. $25-$35.

Goldwater, 1964, Clinton, 1992. Campaign glasses. The Goldwater pair were made intentionally without lenses. $20 and $8 respectively.

Perot, 1992. This is a 50-state set of Perot/Stockdale jugates. There are about 62 known Perot/Stockdale jugates of which these are the majority. $50 to $75 per set, singles $2 to $4.

Douglas MacArthur, 1948, 1952. Many people supported MacArthur's candidacy for president after the war. However, the country's interest in a general shifted to Eisenhower in 1952. MacArthur was on the ballot in some states as a third-party candidate for president but he received only a few thousand votes. Larger buttons are 1-1/4 inch. Top row, $5-$10, $25-$40, $10-$15, $10-$15. Bottom row, $25-$50, $10-$15, $75-$100, $10-$20.

Reagan, 1981. Inaugural license plates are valid in Washington, DC. $8-$15 pair.

Nixon, 1968. The large button is 3 inches. Top row, $5-$10, $4-$6, $25-$35. Bottom row, $3-$8, $3-$5, $4-$8.

Anti-Nixon poster, 1972. One of the most offensive campaign posters ever made. Edge of poster states that it was produced by "Artists' and writers' protest". $5-$10.

Community Party, 1930s. Money collection can $50-$75.

Barry Goldwater, 1964. Novelty doll, $25.

A selection of 1996 buttons. Prices range from $1 to $4 each.

Part II - Types of Items

Kinds of Buttons & Pins

Celluloids

In 1893 a patent was issued to a woman in Boston, Amanda M. Lougee, for a celluloid-covered pinback button. By 1896 the Whitehead and Hoag Co. acquired the patent and began creating the political campaign button as we know it.

The button consisted of a metal shell covered by a paper on which the design was printed and a protective clear celluloid covering. The celluloid was laminated to the paper, which was wrapped around the back of the metal shell and the edge was crimped around a metal ring called a collet which held a pin in place.

Laminates and mylar

More recently celluloid has been replaced by different types of plastic laminates. For small run and home button machines, plastic known as mylar, which is not bonded to the paper, but merely pressed against it, have been used. An unlaminated mylar button is easy to distinguish because the surface of the paper is visible under the plastic. On a laminated button the color of the ink appears to be imbedded in the surface. All of these types of buttons are known to collectors as celluloid buttons, or cellos.

Lithographs

By the 1920s, manufacturers had begun making political buttons by printing right on the metal and not using paper or celluloid. The metal could then be crimped without using a collet. This ability to avoid the paper, celluloid and collet saved considerable labor and money. Unfortunately, the designs which could be printed on the metal surface were much less elaborate than the designs which could be printed on paper. Therefore, the quality of litho button designs have never been as good as celluloids.

While lithographed buttons cost much less to make, they must be made in large quantities because of the high set-up costs. Minimum orders for litho buttons are usually 5000 and often they are made by the hundreds of thousands or even millions. For this reason you would think all litho buttons should be inexpensive. However, many are quite rare and expensive. Were the rest that were made thrown away, or are they sitting in someone's attic or a warehouse somewhere waiting to be discovered?

Because the ink is printed directly on the metal button surface, and they are packaged in bags for distribution, many litho buttons are often scratched and scuffed. In the 1980s lithos were offered with the option of a thin clear plastic coating which makes them appear to be celluloid buttons and protects them from most minor scratches.

Convention badges

Very attractive badges have been issued for political party conventions for over a hundred years. Because most of them are for generic party functions and do not support a particular candidate, they are usually priced very reasonably.

50% $30-$50
RNC 1900

50% $60-$85
RNC 1912

50% $25-$40
DNC 1960

50% $30-$40
RNC 1924

50% $35-$70
RNC 1940

50% $30-$40
RNC 1920

Unusual items

While most current political buttons are nearly identical to their 100-year-old counterparts, some manufacturers have used novel items on their buttons such as moving eyes. In the 1970s and '80s, lights and music were added to buttons. While the expense of making these has kept them from wide distribution, their unusual character should make them key items in any collection. Computers now allow manufacturers to create individual buttons with the candidate along with the purchaser of the button. (This was first done photographically in 1952).

50%   Blinking light $30-$50

50%   Moving eyes $3-$6

50%   Cut from actual dollar bill $8-$12

50%   Purchaser's photo $10-$15

50%   Spinner $3-$5

50%   Blinking light $4-$8

Flashers

A "flasher" is a button which changes its picture depending on the direction from which it is viewed. Flashers were first used for political buttons in the 1950s campaigns of Eisenhower and Stevenson. While they had few adherents for many years and were available for only a few dollars each, they have become more popular and today some command prices of hundreds of dollars.

$20-$25   60% $35-$50

70% $3-$6   60% $20-$40

50% $2-$3   70% $5-$10

Jewelry

Celluloid buttons just aren't fancy enough for formal functions. And with all the formal fund-raisers held to support political candidates, more classy items were needed. Celluloid buttons just don't look good on a nice dress or suit. Thus the development of political jewelry.

$15-$20

$25-$35

$3-$6

$2-$4

$3-$5

$2-$3

Mechanicals

Mechanicals are buttons or trinkets which have moveable parts. These usually display the candidate when you push part of the item. These were most popular around the turn of the century, though they were also made for recent elections. As can be expected, the early ones were intricately made from metal, and the recent ones are made on less expensive materials such as paper.

$60-$90

Sliding loop down switches back
wording to "16 to 1" and causes
eagle to drop head and wing.

$150-$250

$100-$125

50%

Pushing heel causes tail
and arm to appear.

$20-$40

Six and nine inch buttons

Buttons as large as ten inches were made as soon as the button was invented. But both the cost and the awkwardness of the large sizes made them less popular than smaller buttons during campaigns. Some were made with hooks or stands so that they could be mounted on the wall or stood up on a table.

Before the 1960s there were only a few large buttons at most made for a candidate. For some candidates there are none known to exist.

A six inch button makes a great centerpiece for a display of buttons. Some collectors have found a challenge in trying to collect all of the six or nine inch buttons made.

22% $10-$20   22% $5-$8   22% $7-$10

22% $150-$250

25% $175-$275

Tabs

Once overlooked by most collectors as the cheapest and least desirable campaign items, tabs have gained a following among many collectors. Collecting inexpensive items like tabs is a way to have the fun of the search without the expense of many types of collections. Some collectors take up tabs after their primary collection is nearly complete and they need something else to hunt for when they go to button shows.

Most tabs still cost only a dollar or two, but more unusual ones may be $5 or $10, and some have passed the $100 mark.

$35-$50

$125-$175

$10-$15

$30-$40 $1-$2 $5-$10

$1-$3   50¢-$2 $2-$3

Categories of Collectible Items

There are so many types of political items available, the person attempting to collect everything would soon become both overwhelmed and broke. To narrow one's focus and make the goal of completion reachable, most collectors specialize in either a certain candidate such as Roosevelt or Kennedy, or a type of item, such as buttons, bandannas or stamps.

Specializing by candidate

Most collectors have a few favorite candidates whose buttons they collect. These may be candidates whose campaigns they have worked on, or historical figures from the past. Some collect merely because they think the candidate will be a good investment, others because they are grateful for the programs that person started.

On the following pages are some representative items from specialized collections of some popular candidates. These represent only a few of the hundreds of items available for each candidate.

Theodore Roosevelt

Teddy Roosevelt is considered one of our great presidents and the only twentieth century president on Mt. Rushmore. He was a very charismatic figure and is still remembered for his presidential deeds.

Was he greater than the presidents of recent memory? Because he was president before most of us were born we know mostly of his great deeds and not what the opposition said about him. Reading his biography will add life to your collection of his campaign items.

$400-$500 $600-$700

$100-$175 $1000-$2000 $20-$30

$25-$35 $20-$30

James M. Cox

James M. Cox was an Ohio newspaper editor who became the 1920 Democratic presidential nominee just as the country was ready to return to Republican policies. His chief claim to fame in the political collecting hobby is that buttons picturing him and his running mate, the young Franklin Roosevelt, are the rarest and most expensive. Because the campaign was under-financed, the buttons were unattractive and did not represent a winner, even his name buttons are scarce and a collection of Cox buttons is a real accomplishment.

$300-$375 $275-$325

$200-$275 $400-$600

$175-$250 $700-$1200   50% $600-$800

$80-$100 $30-$45 $30-$45 $40-$50

John W. Davis

John W. Davis followed Cox as the 1924 Democratic presidential nominee. The 1924 convention was unusual in that it took a record 108 ballots before a single candidate, Davis, received enough votes to secure the nomination. While Davis-Bryan jugates are cheaper than Cox-Roosevelt jugates, all other Davis buttons are harder to find and more expensive to obtain. Putting together a Davis collection takes patience and a deep pocket.

$700-$1000 $200-$400 $275-$325

$275-$325 $400-$600 $110-$130 $1400-$2200

$160-$220 $175-$200 $100-$200 $75-$125

Franklin D. Roosevelt

As the only president elected to four terms, and the one who ended the Great Depression and started Social Security, Franklin D. Roosevelt enjoys great popularity, at least among those who remember him. With four different campaigns there are numerous items to collect, starting as low as a dollar or two. The late Joseph Jacobs of Chicago spent a lifetime collecting FDR items and still never had them all.

$150-$200

$20-$30

$80-$120

$15-$20

$20-$30

$20-$30

$40-$70

$2-$3

$4-$6

Douglas MacArthur

Although never nominated by a major party, Douglas MacArthur enjoyed much popular support when he returned from World War II. If Eisenhower had not been nominated, MacArthur may have had a better chance. He was a hopeful in at least three elections and was on the ballot in several states in 1952 under at least 4 different third-party designations, but received less than 15,000 votes.

$5-$12 $15-$25 $8-$12 $25-$35

$5-$12 $5-$12 $5-$12 $5-$12

$15-$25 $40-$80 $15-$25

Harry S. Truman

After serving most of Roosevelt's fourth term, Truman had an uphill battle for re-election in 1948. The most popular item from that election is the early edition of the Chicago *Tribune* which declared that Dewey had won. Most expected Dewey to win and many more Dewey campaign items are still available. Even Truman name pins are quite scarce.

$200-$275　　　　　　　$20-$30　　　　　　　$20-$30

$30-$45　　　　　　　$30-$40　　　　　　　$300-$400

$300-$600　　　　　　　$40-$60

Dwight D. Eisenhower

As a hero of World War II, "Ike" had a relatively easy campaign against Governor Adlai Stevenson of Illinois, and numerous items were created to support his campaign. His term in office was during the uneventful 1950s, and some collect his buttons and kitschy items as mementoes of calmer times.

$45-$65

$30-$40

$15-$20

$40-$75

$2-$3

$25-$40

$5-$10

John F. Kennedy

As the leader of "Camelot" and our first martyred president in over 60 years, Kennedy entered the hearts of millions of Americans. Even those who do not collect political items often save some souvenir of his campaign or his assassination. Although not considered as great a president as Lincoln, for many he evokes fond memories and his campaign items will probably remain popular collectibles for many years.

$7-$12   50% $175-$250

$50-$65   Recent novelty $2-$3

$2-$5 $3-$8

Richard M. Nixon

Although Richard Nixon was the first president to resign his office, he still has many followers who feel his accomplishments were much greater than his failings. Nixon was a controversial figure and his five campaigns for national office have left us with thousands of items to collect.

50% $150-$200

70% $5-$10

50% $150-$250

30% $35-$50

$1-$3

$1-$3

50¢-$1

Gerald Ford

The first president who reached the office through appointment rather than election, Gerald Ford's presidency stands out as a unique event in American history. And while his subsequent unsuccessful campaign came at a time when button makers were active, many of his campaign items are unusually hard to find. Many Ford buttons are priced in the $3 to $5 range, and there are hundreds of varieties, but finding them is a challenge.

40% $50-$75   50% $5-$10

$1-$2   70% $5-$20

$1-$3 $2-$4

Ronald W. Reagan

Ronald Reagan is a president who was either loved or hated. The right wing loved him for finally capturing the presidency for their side. The left hated him for reversing public policy the Democrats had been liberalizing for nearly 50 years. His items are still plentiful and his memory still fresh, but watch for his popularity to rise as time passes.

70% $3-$5 $2-$5

70% $4-$8   70% $3-$5

50% $3-$5   70% Lights and music $10-$15

Ross Perot

Ross Perot was a unique phenomenon in American presidential history. By vocalizing complaints held by millions of citizens he was able to build grassroots support for his independent candidacy which was greater than any challenger to the two-party system since Teddy Roosevelt. With most buttons being issued in limited quantities by independent support groups throughout the country, a Perot collection can be a real challenge.

70% $4-$8

70% $3-$6

70% $4-$8

70% $2-$4

50% $10-$20

70% $3-$6

William J. Clinton

Whatever their party, Americans usually have some feelings of support for their leader. With Bill Clinton, there may be stronger negative feelings from the opposition than in years past. The number of anti-Clinton items is unusual. Whether Clinton will be a popular president and his items highly sought-after will not be known for many years.

50% $4-$8   70% $3-$6

70% $2-$4   50% $2-$4

70% $3-$5   70% $2-$4

Jugates

Jugates, items picturing two candidates, are among the most popular of campaign items. The ultimate goal for many collectors is a jugate item for each presidential campaign ticket. If specializing in buttons, it is a lofty goal. A Cox-Roosevelt jugate from 1920 would cost over $20,000 and a Davis-Bryan from 1924 would cost at least $2000.

$30-$50

$1000-$1400

$200-$275

$275-$350

$350-$425

$1-$3

70% $2-$3

70% $2-$3

70% $3-$6

Trigates... and more

An item picturing three persons is called a trigate. One picturing four, a quadragate. Higher numbers are usually made up at will by collectors or simply called multigates. These types of items usually picture the presidential nominee and candidates for lower offices. Usually the lower office candidate creates the item in order to ride on the "coattail" of a popular candidate.

$150-$200

$1000-$1200

70% $1200-$1600

$200-$250

50% $3-$6

70% $5-$20

Single picture

Because jugates for many candidates are not affordable for most new collectors, they often start by collecting single picture pins. For nearly all candidates there are single-picture pins available at reasonable prices.

$20-$35 $20-$35 $10-$20

$8-$15 $15-$25 $3-$8

$1-$3 $3-$8   70% $2-$5

Double Name Buttons

A cross between a jugate and a name button is a button with the names of both the presidential and vice-presidential nominees. Most of these are similar in price to single name buttons and in fact there is a Cox-Roosevelt name button which is cheaper than most single name Cox buttons.

It is interesting to note that while there are numerous types of "Ike and Dick" buttons, there are only a few "Eisenhower and Nixon" buttons.

$30-$45

$160-$220

$5-$10

$2-$3

$3-$8

$1-$2

$1-$2

$1-$2

$1-$2

Single Name Buttons

For starting a collection, name buttons are the most basic buttons to be found. For most candidates of the 20th century the cost is between 50¢ and $5. But for the two toughest, Cox and Davis, the cost will be in the $40 to $75 range.

$10-$20	$40-$50	$75-$150

$1-$3	$2-$3	$2-$5

$1-$3	$1-$2	$1-$2

Slogans

Slogan buttons are very popular with those interested in the historical aspects of the campaigns. Obscure slogans can reveal the important issues of the day. An especially interesting task is attempting to obtain all of the hundreds of varieties of buttons issued in 1940 supporting Wendell Willkie (and opposing Franklin Roosevelt).

$20-$30

$10-20

$60-$80

$300-$400

50%

$15-$20

$3-$7

$1-$2

$3-$6

Graphics

At the present time, well-designed buttons with colorful graphics are among the most popular to collect. Beautiful buttons which cost $25 or $75 a few years ago now command hundreds or even thousands of dollars. If you seek items which make beautiful displays, and are not concerned about cost, these are the ones to collect.

$800-$1200

$5000-$6000

$150-$250

COPYRIGHT 1924 F. H. BUFFUM, JR.

$10-$15

$3500-$4500

$15-$25

60% $10-$20

$300-$400

$4-$8

Inaugurals

Inaugural items are generally not as popular as items used in the campaigns, but specialists in a candidate are often eager collectors of them.

50% $20-$35

70%

$2-$4

$25-$45

50% $3-$8   70% $2-$5

One-day Events

Since one-day event items are only available to a limited number of people for one day, they are often the hardest to find. However, leftover quantities of recent items sometimes make it into the hobby, making them plentiful.

$1000-$1700 $400-$600   50% $25-$35

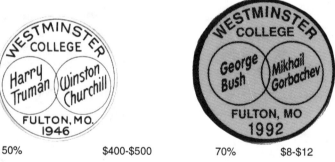

50% $400-$500   70% $8-$12

$5-$15   50% $275-$350   70% $3-$5

Hopeful Candidates

Those who sought their party's presidential nomination but lost are called "hopefuls." Some people specialize in the buttons of hopefuls. While there are many more candidates than actual nominees, most hopefuls had only a few buttons issued for their candidacy so a collection of hopefuls would be smaller than a collection of nominees. However, a few candidates, such as Edward M. Kennedy, had hundreds of buttons issued supporting their candidacy.

$15-$20

$7-$12

$2-$5

70% $10-$20

70% $1-$3

70% $1-$2

70% $2-$4

70% $2-$5

Third Parties

In the 1950s and '60s, third party buttons were among the most popular to collect. They are still highly sought-after, and an ideal collection would consist of one jugate from each party for each election.

$700-$1200

$75-$100

$25-$35

$25-$40

$35-$50

$4-$8

$3-$8   70% $1-$3

70% $4-$8

Sets

Throughout the years manufacturers have released sets of buttons with common designs but different wording. The most common sets are for different states, languages or nationalities.

While recent sets may come on the market with relative frequency at reasonable prices, sets before 1968 must be acquired one button at a time and are a real challenge to assemble.

$30-$60

$15-$30

$8-$20

$10-$15

$10-$25

$3-$6

$3-$6

$2-$4

Candidates' Early Career Items

Many of our presidential candidates did not win on their first try. They lost a few times before winning the big one. And as a loser, their buttons were not considered very valuable so most were probably thrown away.

Consider Ronald Reagan. There are countless buttons available in large quantities from his 1980 and 1984 elections. But how often does a 1968 Reagan button come along? Or a 1972 Reagan? (Yes, there were at least 5 different types made, even though Nixon had a lock on the nomination.) And many were made for his 1976 attempt to wrest the nomination from President Ford. There is even a button and a stamp from Reagan's days as a Hollywood personality, and many gubernatorial items.

Nixon was elected to the House and lost both the presidency (1960) and the governorship of California (1962) before winning the presidency in 1968. John F. Kennedy was elected to the House and Senate, Truman ran for Judge and the Senate. Even Abraham Lincoln lost a few campaigns before winning the presidency. Their early buttons are sleeping gems waiting to be discovered and appreciated.

$50-$150

$300-$400

$1500-$2500

$275-$325

$20-$30

$8-$20

Candidates' Future Possibilities

While most former presidents do not try to make a come-back (Grover Cleveland and Teddy Roosevelt being notable exceptions) their supporters often pine for their return. "He's tan, rested and ready - Nixon in '88" was perhaps the most unexpected.

$5-$15

$2-$5

$2-$6

$2-$4

$2-$3

$2-$3

"Anti" Items

Some of the most clever and interesting buttons are those made in opposition to a candidate. Clever slogans and graphics are often used and the candidates own words or actions have been turned around in ridicule.

$100-$200

This is an anti-JFK button issued $75-$125
during the 1960 campaign.

$5-$15

$75-$125

50% $5-$15

$2-$5

70% $2-$5

Women's Rights...(and Men's)

Votes for woman (suffrage) items are among the rarest of campaign items. In recent years some determined collectors have bid them up to astronomical levels. More recent women's rights items are still reasonably priced as are men's rights items.

$500-$800

$150-$250

$1000-$1700

$2-$4

$500-$800

$20-$30

70% $2-$4   70% $2-$4   70% $2-$4

Causes

Many political causes have inspired campaign items and these are also hot collectibles, though often less expensive than presidential items of the same era.

Prohibition

$10-$20

$20-$30

$10-$20

Civil Rights

$3-$5

70% $3-$5

70% $3-$5

70% $3-$5

Anti-war and Win the War

50% $3-$10

$2-$5

70% $2-$5

70% $1-$3

Drugs

70% $3-$8

$3-$8

Abortion

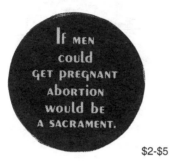

$2-$5

$2-$5

$2-$5

70% $2-$5

Anti-government

70% "B.A.T.F." (Waco) $2-$3

$3-$5

$1-$3

First Ladies

There are few First Lady items produced, and they are usually not expensive, so the cost of collecting them is relatively reasonable. However, it is a challenge to find them. One interesting fact is that while there are many anti-Eleanor Roosevelt items, there are no known buttons supportng her.

$35-$45

50% $50-$100

70% $5-$10

50% $50-$75

50% $40-$70   70% $2-$5

Support Groups

Various groups have issued buttons supporting a particular candidate. Some of these are very scarce because the groups were small.

$3-$8

$30-$40

70%　　　　$3-$5

$2-$5

50%　　　　$4-$8

$5-$10

Fantasy Groups

Transvestite Bobsledders for Kerry? Adultrous[sic] Televangelists for Clinton? Some buttons were obviously not issued by actual groups to support candidates. They were put out by button manufacturers for fun or to ridicule a candidate. Will they ever be worth anything? A button with the slogan "Prostitutes... vote for Nixon or Kennedy We don't care who gets in!" has sold for over $300.

$90-$150 $100-$200 $2-$5

$2-$4 $3-$8

70% $3-$8   70% $3-$5   50% $3-$8

Novelty Buttons

Collectors are the main market for some manufacturers, so buttons are designed which are clever, enough to inspire a $2 impulse buy, but which would probably not be worn by any supporters (except, perhaps, at a button collectors' convention).

$30-$60

$4-$8

70% $2-$5

70% $2-$5

70% $3-$5

$2-$5

Locals

With each of the major presidential nominees inspiring hundreds of buttons, and older buttons rising to unprecedented price levels, more collectors than ever are taking up the collecting of items for candidates for state offices. Some collect only their own state. Others specialize in a certain time period, or interest such as women or African-American candidates.

The most popular are senator and governor buttons. Items for other offices such as congress and mayor are usually collected only by people in those states or cities.

While there may be several candidates for governor and senator, each usually has only one or a few buttons, and the lower demand keeps the prices of these reasonable.

International items

There are so many American political items to collect, and so few foreign items to be found in this country, that very few collectors take up collecting foreign items.

One exception is Soviet pins. During the Soviet regime, Russia and some of the other countries in eastern Europe issued hundreds, or possibly thousands of pins celebrating the Soviet system. Most likely these were used to keep the youth interested in communism and amused enough to forget their dire straights.

In recent years some of these items pictured or named U. S. presidents and collectors who specialize in those presidents are eager to obtain Soviet pins with their hero.

The author does not know of any catalog of foreign political items, so adding these to your collection would be a real challenge.

Reagan/ $10-$15
Gorbachev

Bush/ $5-$15
Gorbachev

$2-$5

$3-$6

$2-$5

Mao (China) $5-$10   (Poland) $2-$5   Havel(Czech.) $5-$10

Paper Items

Stamps

Political campaign stamps seem to get little respect. Stamp collectors don't consider them stamps, and political collectors do not consider them as desirable as buttons. Some rare examples have sold for up to $400, but most are underpriced compared to their scarcity and graphic appeal.

$5-$10

$1-$3

$4-$6

$1.50-$3

$3-$5

50¢-$1

50¢-$1

$1-$2

Stationary and Envelopes

Stationary and envelopes are usually inexpensive to obtain, unless they are postmarked, in which case they are desirable to stamp collectors. For example, unused Abraham Lincoln envelopes sell for a fraction of what used ones do. But as political collectors seek out the unused ones, their value is rising.

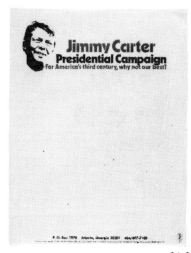

$25-$50 $20-$30

$15-$25

$1-$2

50¢-$1

Inaugural Covers

Since at least 1929, collectors have made up special envelopes to be cancelled on inauguration day. The post office began using a special cancellation, and in recent elections has made them available in several locations including the president's and vice-president's birthplaces.

Collectors and vendors have designed artwork for these covers, called cachets, and many collectors attempt to obtain all cachets for a particular candidate.

$2-$4

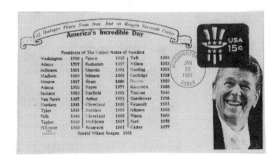

$2-$4

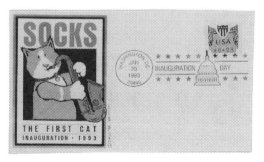

$2-$4

Stickers

Campaign stickers (peel-and-stick, rather than lick and stick stamps) have been even less popular than campaign stamps. One problem is that the glue migrates through the paper causing unsightly stains. Fortunately, solvents can be used to dissolve the glue and restore the stickers to their original look. With many campaigns today using stickers instead of buttons, look for these to become more popular.

$3-$8

50¢-$1

$1-$2

$1-$3

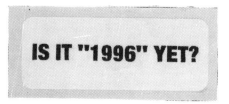

50¢-$1

Window stickers

Few people specialize in collecting window stickers, but those who collect particular candidates eagerly seek them, and stickers with good graphics or slogans are in demand by many collectors.

$3-$6

$10-$20

$3-$5

$5-$10

$5-$10

$6-$10

$3-$5

$1-$3

Bumper stickers

Bumper stickers also have few specialists, and again the most eager collectors seek a special candidate.

$2-$4

NIXON'S THE ONE!

$1-$3

$1-$3

Remember
October 9

$1-$3

$1-$3

REAGAN ★
FOR REASON ★

$1-$3

$1-$2

Trading cards

Political trading cards probably have more adherents among non-sports card collectors in the trading card world than in the political hobby. Consequently, you can probably get more bargains at a political collectors' convention, and expect to pay more at a trading card convention.

$15-$25 $15-$25 $3-$5

$3-$5 $3-$10 $1-$3

$2-$4 $3-$5 $1-$3

Tickets and Invitations

There are specialists in political convention tickets (and a catalog for them will be published in 1997 by Noble Publishing), so they are not as cheap as many paper items. But for their age and beauty they are bargains. Other event tickets are relatively inexpensive.

$3-$6

$50-$150

$5-$15

$1-$4

50¢-$1

Mock Currency

Political campaign currency, that is, political leaflets designed like currency, have many adherents but are still relatively inexpensive and easy to find. Besides political shows, they can be found at coin and currency shows as well as paper and ephemera shows.

$50-$100

$5-$20

$1-$3

$1-$3

50¢-$1

Post Cards

There is such a large group of post card collectors that political post cards are much more expensive than most political paper items. Rare cards can fetch thousands of dollars. Most postcard dealers have their stock well organized and researched, so bargains are rare at post card shows.

$20-$40

$2-$4

$15-$25

$1-$3

$1-$3

Catalogs

Seeing $700 campaign pins priced at $7.50 per gross and $300 lanterns priced at 80¢ a dozen in a 1900 catalog is enough to make a grown collector cry. Why didn't our grandparents stash away a few dozen? But catalogs of old campaign items are interesting collectibles. The fact that many items pictured in the catalogs are not found in any collection makes one wonder how many more items are waiting to be discovered.

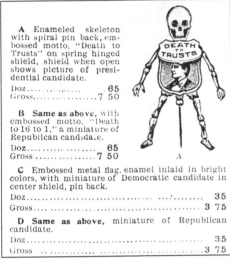

A Enameled skeleton with spiral pin back, embossed motto, "Death to Trusts" on spring hinged shield, shield when open shows picture of presidential candidate.

Doz.... .. .,..... .65
Gross,................7 50

B Same as above, with embossed motto, "Death to 16 to 1," a miniature of Republican candidate.

Doz.................. 65
Gross 7 50

C Embossed metal flag, enamel inlaid in bright colors, with miniature of Democratic candidate in center shield, pin back.

Doz................................. ...:..... 35
Gross...3 75

D Same as above, miniature of Republican candidate.

Doz... 35
Gross 3 75

Ad from a 1900 campaign material catalog. Entire catalog $50-$80

$10-$20

$5-$10

13/16" Pin-on Button Two Colors	**BUTTONS**	
ITEM NO.	1,000	5,000
#15	$12.00M	$ 9.50M

1" Pin-on Buttons
Two Colors

1" Dia. Metal Litho Button

PRICES	
1.000	5.000
15.00 per M	13.00 per M

Buttons are packed 1000 to bag.
See ordering information

B (⅞")	13.50M

Part of a 1964 flier. $3-$5

Sheet Music

Some people specialize in sheet music, but probably the most demand for these items comes from specialists in a candidate.

$300-$700

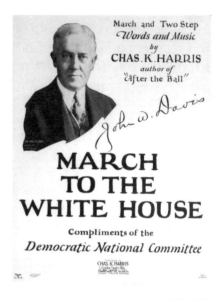

$40-$60

$75-$110

$3-$6

Posters

While some collectors feel that political campaign posters are too large to enjoy, others use them as home or office decorations. Because their size is a handicap to many, posters well over a hundred years old are still available at very reasonable prices.

The most reasonably priced posters were originally distributed as supplements to magazines and newspapers of the day. Because these were preserved in large quantities by both libraries and individuals, excellent copies can be found easily. Actual campaign posters, especially jugates, are more difficult to find.

$50-$100

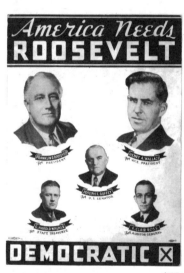

$75-$125

$5-$10

Newspapers

Newspapers are not especially popular among political collectors except for those seeking a special candidate. Prices are usually in the $5 to $15 range, even for papers nearly 200 years old. Two exceptions are shown below, headline errors, along with a common issue.

$200-$300

$400-$700

$2-$4

Brochures

Campaign brochures are among the least popular of campaign items and are very inexpensive. Again specialists in a candidate are the most interested parties

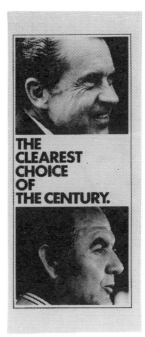

$2-$6   50¢-$1

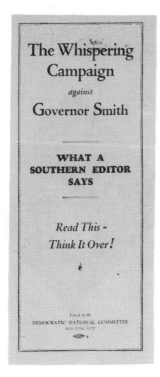

$3-$10

$2-$5

Textiles

Textile items are among the most attractive items in museum exhibits, yet because they require a lot of space to exhibit and store, they are not in as great demand among collectors. For this reason they are still available at very reasonable prices.

Bandannas, Scarves and Handkerchiefs

$200-$250 $40-$50

$30-$60 $30-$60

Clothing

Clothing items make great display items if you have the room. You can buy a mannikin to display your Ike nylons, McCarthy dress, Nixon hat and various jewelry.

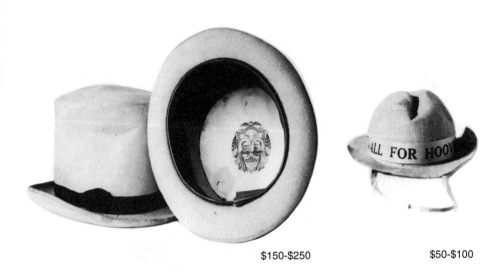

$150-$250

$50-$100

$25-$50 $45-$65

Flags and Pennants

The best campaign flags are from the last century, however, there are many pennants available for candidates from the twentieth century and the prices are very reasonable.

$25-$50

$80-$100

$7-$15

Ribbons

The most colorful and desirable ribbons are from the 19th century. Often they were made in multi-colored designs with pictures of the candidates. Recent ribbons are usually one color with gold printing and sell for only a few dollars.

$60-$90 $45-$75 $1-$2

3-D Items

For some, three-dimensional items are the most exciting political collectibles. Old campaign torches and lanterns, and new toys and banks are pieces of Americana which are seldom seen outside of museums. But because they are bulky and difficult to transport and store, they attract fewer collectors and seem underpriced compared to other items of similar age. They are especially useful if you display your collection in a local library or school.

Novelty items

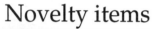

McKinley bar of soap, $60-$100

Taft-Sherman metal dish
$80-$120

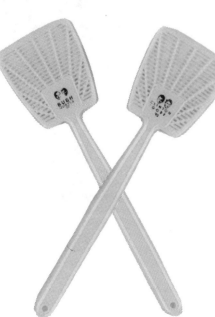

Bush-Quayle and Clinton-Gore
jugate flyswatters, $3-$6 each.

Full dinner pail jar. $350-$450

More novelty items

Condom, $3-$5

Bar of soap, $25-$40

$3-$5

JFK bubblegum cigar box, $50-$60

Clicker $10-$20

Bag of candy, $3-$5

Fobs

Fobs were ornaments worn at the end of a pocket watch strap. Because pocket watches are not used much any more, fobs have declined in popularity. Several years ago a large hoard of Cox-Roosevelt and Harding-Coolidge jugate fobs were found and these may be used as a relatively inexpensive substitute for the jugate buttons.

$50-$75 $60-$90 $20-$35

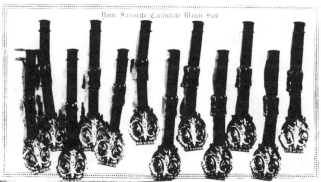

Complete card of Cox-Roosevelt jugate fobs $80-$125 each

Glassware and Food-related Items

Glassware is very popular among collectors of 3-D items. Because of its fragility, fewer pieces exist each year, therefore the values rise steadily.

$150-$200

$75-$150

$5-$10

$15-$25

$10-$20

$8-$15

$5-$10

Knives

Pocket knives also have aficionados outside the political hobby and can be found at many gun shows and other collectibles shows. Like the button, the Cox-Roosevelt jugate is the prize.

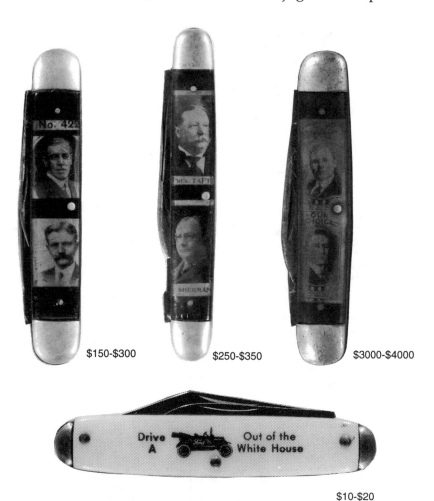

$150-$300 $250-$350 $3000-$4000

$10-$20

$3-$6

License plates and attachments

Because license plates and attachments become rusted and damaged when used on a car, good quality specimens are especially valuable. License plate collectors may pay more for inaugural plates than political collectors.

$75-$125

$100-$150

$30-$60

$125-$200

$40-$60

$75-$125

$100-$200

Pens and Pencils

Writing implements have been used for campaigns for over 100 years and are still relatively inexpensive. Once again, most are sought by specialists in a candidate.

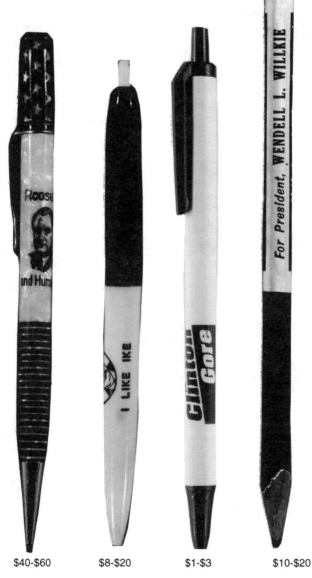

$40-$60 $8-$20 $1-$3 $10-$20 $1-$3

Smoking-related items

The decline in smoking among Americans, and the prolif-eration of inexpensive lighters has caused a decline in the number of advertising matchbooks used. But many smoking items have been produced for political campaigns over the years.

$20-$40

$25-$50

$5-$10

$10-$20

50¢-$2

50¢-$2

50¢-$2

Part III - Collecting Political Items

Where to Find Political Items

Political Collectibles Shows

The best place to find a good selection of political items at a fair price is from other collectors at political collectibles shows. These are held all over the country throughout the year and offer an unbelievable variety of all types of items. Smaller shows might have 10 or 20 tables but regional and national shows have 100 to 300 tables. Nearly all of the dealers and collectors at the events have scoured their area for political items to bring to these shows. A few have dug out their collections after many years of inactivity and decided to dispose of them.

While it takes time and money to travel to these shows, it is well worth it for the serious collector. Many collectors take time off work and fly across the country to attend these shows because the opportunity is so great to obtain good items at a fair price. Often a few bargains can more than pay for all of your expenses. Knowledgeable collectors have been able to buy, sell and trade items at the same show and make enough profit to pay for the trip.

Price lists and ads by collectors

Many collectors of political items finance their collection by dealing in political items. If their local antique dealer has three identical Kennedy buttons, they don't buy just one for their collection, they get all three and sell the extras. Since prices are so fluid, it is easy to make a profit on items you buy, either immediately, or a few years later.

Display ads in the political collectibles newspapers (see Appendix 1 for names and addresses) picture numerous items for sale, and classified ads offer photocopied lists of hundreds of items.

Auctions

For items costing $20 and up, political button auctions are a good place to buy. Because of the volatility of prices, auctions are sometimes the only place one can hope to find an item.

Comparing auctions with shows, the prices will often be considerably higher at auctions. But more and more good items are showing up only in auctions rather than shows because the owners hope to get a higher price at the auctions where hundreds of collectors must bid against each other.

Auction fever can be a problem for rare items. Often key items will go for double or triple their estimated value, if two or more bidders "must have" the item to complete their collection and do not want to wait five years for another to surface. Occasionally the same item will be in another auction six months later and cost only half its previous high because only one serious collector is left who needs it.

But there will also be bargains at auctions. With hundreds or thousands of items to choose from, many items which appear regularly in the auctions do not get any bids, and can be picked up reasonably. Don't expect to steal the items. If the only bid on a $20 item is $2 the auctioneer or consignor will either withdraw the items or bid himself. But some items can be bought for 80 or even 70 percent of the estimate.

The larger political shows usually have one or two auctions. One usually consists of items consigned by the members. Many rare and unusual items appear at these auctions and often the prices are very reasonable.

Antique stores and flea markets

Local antique stores can offer both the best deals and the worst deals in political items. Because of the lack of knowledge of most dealers they often price items by their "gut feeling." This may mean an old button, a colorful one, or one for a popular figure has a high price and a new button, an ugly one, or one for someone they have never heard of is priced low. Because of this, a dealer may have a common Nixon button (which is worth 50¢), and a rare Davis button (worth $500) both priced at $10.

One danger of buying at antique stores and flea markets is fakes. While attendees of political shows are forbidden from selling such items, no such rules apply to others. Until you become knowledgeable about political items be careful about buying expensive items from antique and flea market dealers. More information on fakes is included in a later chapter.

Many antique and flea market dealers are starting to discover the political item reference catalogs on the market and this can be either good or bad for the collector. It can eliminate the great bargains, but also the overpricing. Because some items have risen in price rapidly, the prices even in recent catalogs may be low. But most dealers ignore the comments in the catalogs about condition and think their badly damaged items are still worth the figure in the catalog which applies to an item in good condition.

Advertising

Many collectors have luck advertising to buy items in local newspapers, shoppers, antique publications and various collectibles publications. Those with special interests often advertise in the political collectors' newspapers. The author has had some luck advertising in the hometown newspaper of various candidates, and in towns where special events took place and one-day buttons were issued.

Political Headquarters

The days are gone when you could walk into a political campaign headquarters and grab a handful of buttons out of a bowl. Buttons are expensive and the money is believed to be better spent on television spots. For rallies, some candidates even substitute paper stickers for buttons (see page 132). Some candidates sell their buttons or only give them to donors. Many headquarters have no buttons at all.

But don't neglect stopping in your local headquarters, You might get lucky. Some local groups create their own buttons and you may end up with the only ones in the hobby.

Occasionally special buttons will be issued for staff members, volunteers or contributors. Sometimes these are also given away freely, other times the staff guards them with their lives. You should ask if there are any special limited-edition buttons. If you bring along some other colorful buttons for the candidate, or even earlier inexpensive Kennedy or Reagan buttons you might be able to trade for a rare staff button. Some collectors even volunteer to work on the campaign in order to get a rare button.

Some people have luck writing to campaign headquarters. Including a stamped, self-addressed (padded) envelope might increase your chances, but if they don't have any buttons you will have wasted your postage. Some collectors invest in a phone call to important headquarters to ask what is available.

Keep in mind that there are headquarters for specific candidates, for groups supporting certain candidates, and for the party organizations. Any of these might have unusual or rare buttons.

The Federal Election Commission (FEC) has the addresses of all candidates' headquarters available as public records. Many collectors have requested the list and had good luck writing to the addresses listed. The FEC does not yet have a web page, but CNN lists the FEC addresses at:

http://www.allpolitics.com/candidates/list.shtml

Fairs

During an election year, state and county fairs usually have booths for political candidates. These are often stocked with buttons and sometimes have locally-produced buttons not available elsewhere.

Political Conventions

Political conventions can be one of the best places to get buttons and other campaign memorabilia. After they are over, collectors have brought home bags and boxes of thousands of items for years of future trading.

At political conventions you can find items put out by political organizations and by numerous vendors. At the national conventions many state delegations put out their own buttons, and every street corner around the convention site may have vendors selling buttons. At the 1992 Republican convention there was a hall off the convention floor just for vendors who sold all types of political souvenirs. Keep in mind that there are third party national conventions and state and local political conventions.

Many rare and limited edition buttons can be found at conventions and many collectors spend a week at both of the major party national nominating conventions. A key way to get good buttons is to trade for them. Delegates who were given boring-looking, but rare, buttons for their delegation often will trade them for a more colorful or older button.

The World Wide Web

Just as television once revolutionized campaigning, many feel the internet will soon do the same. Most candidates in the current race for the White House and many local political groups have web sites. These sites typically give the position of the candidate on the issues, a list of those who have endorsed the candidate, and some even include instructions for ordering buttons and other campaign items.

To enter the world wide web you need a computer, a modem and membership in an online service such as America Online or Compuserve. To find them just use their "web browser" to access any search engine and enter "presidential election" or "presidential campaign" and the sites listed will lead you to more and more sites.

The following are some sites which were current at the time of publication of this book:

Harry Browne for President:
    http: //www.harrybrowne96.org/

Pat Buchanan for President:
        http: //www.buchanan.org/

Bruce Daniels for President:
        http: //www.daniels.winnipeg.mb.ca/

Democratic National Committee:
        http: //www.democrates.org/

Democratic Activists Home Page:
        http: //www.webcom.com/~digitals/

Bob Dole for President:
        http: //www.dole.com/

Independent Candidates Page:
        http: //www.competition96.com/

Libertarian Party:
        http: //www.rahul.net/lp/

Republican National Committee:
        http: //www.rnc.org/

Republicans Web Central:
        http: //www.gop.org/

United We Stand America:
        http: //www.uwsa.org/

Vote Smart Web:
        http: //www.vote-smart.org/

White House:
        http: //www.whitehouse.gov/

Vendor vs. "Official" Items

Since the 1960s there has been a debate within the hobby concerning the relative value of "official" versus "vendor" campaign items. There is a small group of collectors which feels that the only political items worth collecting are so-called "official" items. These collectors shun anything that was made by a commercial vendor for sale to the public, and especially items made by collectors. They feel so strongly about their position that they would expell anyone who made buttons from the collectors' organization, APIC.

The problem with this position is the most beautiful (and valuable) items ever made were vendor items, and the arguments against them are spurious.

What are Vendor Items?

Vendor items are political items designed and manufactured by a private company to sell to the general public and to campaign organizations. The first vendor campaign items were produced for the 1840 election and they have been made ever since then. We can find catalogs and ads in newspapers for nearly every campaign showing numerous campaign items offered by private vendors. One catalog was distributed by the Republican party in 1956 listing private vendors of various items available to its local chapters. Even when ads cannot be found, when campaign items are found in matched sets we can see that they were not designed by one party, but by an independent vendor for sale to both parties.

The Abraham Lincoln photo pins, the beautiful multicolored buttons of the "Golden Age" of buttons, nearly all jugates, and the most creative buttons of nearly every campaign were all "unofficial" and sold by private vendors for a profit.

What are "Official" Items?

"Official" buttons, on the other hand, are those conceived and/or authorized by some campaign committee or support group. They are often plain, colorless and sometimes ugly. But the collector of "official" buttons finds more joy in obtaining a small two-color button from a small union than from a clever multicolored cartoon button produced by a vendor.

A good example of an official button is the "Nixon Now" litho button from 1972. These were made by the millions and given away freely by Nixon's re-election committee. Most collectors have a bag full and there are enough around for every collector who will ever be born.

The Obsession of Completeness

Why do some collectors shun "unofficial buttons"? Partly for financial reasons. Some vendor items are made in limited quantities and sold at ridiculous prices. For many collectors, completeness becomes not just a goal, but an obsession. Part of the fun of collecting is working toward the goal of a complete collection, and getting a little closer to that goal every few weeks or months keeps the hobby exciting.

If anyone can make a single political button and price it at, say, $100, the obsessed collector is at their mercy. Either he gets ripped off, or his collection will *never be complete*. Completeness is so important to some collectors that the proliferation of vendor buttons has caused them to give up collecting modern buttons.

Collector-Made Buttons

At some point in the evolution of the hobby of political button collecting, some collector realized that if he had a button designed and manufactured, he would be able to trade those buttons for buttons he needed for his collection. Eventually he realized that since he was the only source for that button, he could ask whatever he wanted and those collectors obsessed with completeness would have to pay his price.

This caused an uproar in the hobby. Collectors realized that if every collector could make his own button and ask ridiculous prices it would be hard for anyone to have a complete collection. And what if some collectors made only one or two copies of a button? Those would then be the rarest buttons in the hobby. Some predicted that this would cause the total collapse of the hobby, since no one could have a *complete collection.*

To avoid this catastrophe strict ethical rules were promulgated by the APIC. No collector was allowed to create political buttons unless he was part of an official campaign organization and then he had to disclose his affiliation and could only keep one-half of 1% of the buttons.

Yet collectors still made buttons. In the 1950s and 1960s two popular areas of collecting were jugates and third party buttons. But the small parties were not producing these buttons. Who do you think made all the jugates for such obscure parties as the Greenback Party and the Vegetarian Party? Members, or friends of members, of APIC.

Collector-made buttons really blossomed in 1968. That year, due to the youth movement for Eugene McCarthy and the general political excitement of the time, many more people started collecting political buttons. As usual the parties produced dull and boring buttons. At the Nixon headquarters you could get red and white "Nixon's the One!" buttons in three (small) sizes.

But the vendors of the day filled the need with hundreds of buttons in all sizes, colors and shapes. These were sold at very reasonable prices and were available in adequate quantities for all who wanted them.

Still the "purists" in the hobby complained that these buttons were "unofficial" and "junk" and would ruin the hobby. At least one manufacturer, some of whose buttons are now classics, was expelled from APIC. Other manufacturers, who had been in the button business for many years, were told they could not join the APIC. Every person on the planet could make a political button except a member of APIC. An affidavit was distributed to all dealers by the APIC, but to the disappointment of the officers, their lawyers pointed out that it would violate anti-trust laws.

Shortly after the 1968 election things did somewhat get out of hand. In designing buttons for 1972, manufacturers realized that one design could be printed in 5 or more colors of ink and that at least 10 colors of paper were available. This meant that a single piece of artwork could result in 50 different buttons, including such garish and unreadable combinations as green on yellow and red on dark green.

As America's interest in politics declined after Watergate, so did the frenzy of collector-made buttons. It did not pick up again until 1992 when Americans again were excited by the prospect of a serious third party candidate and Democrats were excited by the first chance in years of regaining the White House. In this excitement many APIC members began making buttons. By November, 1992 it was joked at an APIC convention that the new rule was that a member would be expelled if he *didn't* produce a button.

While many members felt that it didn't matter who made buttons, a majority of the board of directors still wanted to limit what members could make. A new ethics rule was approved in 1995 which forbids members from making items "primarily to sell or trade to collectors."

Should You Collect "Vendor" Buttons?

Today few collectors try to obtain every button, there are just too many. What most do is collect a representative sample of each candidate. Even those who specialize in a single candidate feel free to pass on overpriced items without obsessing over completeness.

The fact is, the best items from most campaigns have nearly all been vendor buttons and 20 years after an election is over few people care. They want the most interesting and attractive buttons from the campaign. Vendor buttons which were shunned at 25¢ during the campaign have passed the $100 mark years later.

The best answer is to collect what you like and find attractive, and buttons that give some special insight to the issues of the campaign. Most vendor buttons are priced very reasonably, and some will be classics some day.

If you see someone asking $25 or $100 for a button for the current election, be wary. It might be a classic some day, but there might be 499 more of them put away for the manufacturer's children's college fund.

Understanding Pricing and Value

The values of political items are not as clear as those of such other collectibles as stamps and coins. This is because the quantities made of most political items is unknown, the collector demand is not as deep as for stamps and coins, and there is not a simple way for all sellers and buyers to find each other.

With stamps and coins the printings and mintages are known precisely, and prices are tracked annually and even weekly by catalogs and newsletters. With political items, not all items are known, quantities made are unknown, and some items come up for sale only once every several years.

This situation helps makes the hobby more exciting. It is not unusual to sell an item for double, triple, or even ten times what you paid for it once you become knowledgable. But it also adds some risk due to price volatility. Some of the best buttons are only known to exist in quantities of a few dozen. If a few wealthy new collectors start bidding in auctions, they could cause the value of those pins to quickly double or triple. But if several old-time collectors decide it is time to sell, or if a handful is discovered in an attic, the price could suddenly drop.

Happily for those who consider their collection an investment, such drops are short term. Discoveries of rare buttons tend to depress prices for a time, but eventually the hobby absorbs all of the find and prices begin to exceed their old levels. Lately, discoverers of hoards of buttons have been clever enough to let them dribble out slowly over the years. Yet no one can keep such an exciting find a complete secret and rumors get out.

The best way to avoid overpaying for political items is to follow the items you like before buying them. After a few months of watching ads and auctions you will know whose prices are fair and what levels your favorite buttons usually reach.

Ted Hake's three volume *Encyclopedia of Political Buttons* is the most comprehensive listing of political items available and the 1991 price guide is relatively accurate. But prices change so quickly that no catalog could give you a completely accurate value.

If a person has a handful of an item he may price it below the catalog value to sell them quickly. If a button has not been seen for sale for many years a seller may ask double the catalog price.

In starting a collection a collector usually buys every item he finds, as long as the price is not unreasonable. After some experience, and numerous discoveries of items at lower prices than he originaly paid, a collector often decides to shop a while to see who has the best price. This can lead to the disappointment of losing the chance to buy an item.

Happily, unless you ridiculously overpay for political items, you will eventually at least get your money back and in most cases make a handsome profit. One political collector, who is also a stock broker, sometimes shows his clients how much more they could make investing in political buttons.

As the ads say, "past performance is no guaranty of future results." But, except for some temporary dips in the market, political campaign items have steadily risen in value, year after year. With supplies of good items limited to begin with, prices rise almost yearly as new collectors enter the hobby. Some buttons which sold for $25 and $50 twenty years ago sell for $500 to $1200 today. A price list from seven years ago has prices one-half to one-quarter what they are today.

One important factor to keep in mind is that most prices quoted for buttons are for those in good condition. A crack or a stain on a button could cut its value in half or even make it worth only 1/10th the value of a mint item. Fading, separation of the celluloid from the paper or rim, rust, and scratches all lessen the value of a button. Tears, holes and adhesive tape stains lower the value of paper and cloth items.

The bottom line is, careful shopping will save a lot of money but don't be afraid to buy what you like, it will usually go up in value.

Care and Storage

Most collectors keep their button collections in thin black boxes with glass tops. These are commonly known as "Riker mounts" or butterfly boxes. They are about 3/4 of an inch deep and filled with cotton or a similar substance. They are available through ads in political periodicals or through the APIC. The most popular sizes are 12 x 16 inches and 8 x 12 inches.

Campaign stamps, stickers, and other small paper items can be mounted on pages made for stamp or baseball card collectors. Be sure any items of this type that you buy are of archival quality and will not damage the items. Do not use wax-based photo albums (sometimes called "magnetic") or anything that was not made for collectibles or your collection may be destroyed.

Duplicate buttons offered for sale are also kept in Riker mounts, or in 3-ring binders. The 3-ring binders can be used with vinyl coin pages and 2x2 holders or with cardboard pages. When using cardboard or paper with buttons, be sure to buy only acid-free paper or the paper will cause the buttons to rust. Acid-free paper and cardboard is available through archival supply houses.

For those with large quantities of duplicates, the above methods may require too much work or expense. Most collectors keep their quantity items in plastic bags or in drawers in plastic parts cabinets. **Warning:** Litho buttons are very easily scratched by each other. For this reason they should be mounted on paper or cardboard as soon as you acquire them. Some collectors mount litho buttons on sheets of plastic.

To remove dirt and restore the lustre to celluloid buttons, many collectors use a product called Simichrome cream. It greatly enhances the appearance of the buttons and occasionally can restore a damaged-looking button to new. But do not use it on litho buttons or on celluloid buttons with cracks or pinholes or it will cause damage.

Your most valuable buttons should be kept in a safe deposit box at a bank. In order to still enjoy them you can make color photocopies of them which can be cut out and put in the trays at home with your cheaper buttons.

Safes

Since most common burglars do not know the value of political items, you might not need a safe, but if you have a valuable collection you might want the extra protection a safe offers. Because of the risk of a broken water pipe or flooding, an in-floor safe is not a good idea. For a quantity of Riker mounts a large gun safe is ideal.

Beware of fire safes. The way fire safes work is to release water on the contents when the heat rises. This could permanently damage your collection. Better to place the safe in a corner against a concrete wall where risk of fire is lowest. But a basement or garage is dangerous because the humidity and temperature changes could damage the items.

Insurance

It may be difficult to get adequate coverage for your collection under a standard homeowner's or tenant's policy. It is important that you confirm with your insurance agent that your collection is covered for its full value. It may have to be specifically listed.

If you cannot insure it through your policy, and a separate policy through your agent is too expensive, there are other options. The American Philatelic Society (a stamp collectors' group) offers insurance to its members at a very reasonable rate, and recently the policies were amended to include buttons and ephemera. The amount saved on insurance could more than pay for the dues. The address of the APS is included in Appendix 1.

For collections valued at over $100,000, APIC has found an agent who can write a policy for a political button collection. While the underwriter is not writing individual collectibles policies in some states, this agent is able to write policies for those who are members of APIC.

Fakes and Reproductions

Like most collectibles which have become valuable, rare political buttons have been counterfeited. But the number of such items is small, most are easy to detect, and nearly all have been listed in a booklet published by the American Political Items Collectors.

If you get this booklet and learn a little about the items you are collecting there is very little chance you will get stuck with a fake item.

One exception is Washington inaugural buttons. These are brass coat buttons and many copies of these were made in the 1800s. When purchasing these items be sure to deal with a reputable dealer who will guaranty the item.

The most common fake buttons were manufactured as advertising give-aways by Kleenex and the American Oil Co. These are sets of buttons with one for each candidate from the Democratic and Republican parties. While the recent ones look similar to real buttons, the older ones are obvious fakes because they are lithographed, whereas lithographs did not exist before about 1920. Another giveaway is that on the back edge they usually state "AO-1972" or "repro 1968," or " reproduction."

"REPRODUCTION" ——   —— "EISENHOWER 1956"

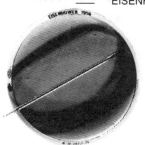

———————— "A-O-1972-31"

Fakes from these sets can be found in many antique stores and often unscrupulous owners have either scratched off or painted over the inscription on the edge. Some have even intentionally caused them to rust to try to trick buyers into thinking they are old.

Fantasies

While a fake button is a copy of a real button, a fantasy is a button which never existed during the campaign. These are modern creations made to look like old buttons, but designed without copying a real button.

If you come across a button which is not in any catalog or auction there is a chance that you have found a rare undiscovered variety, but also a chance that you have come across a fantasy button. Check with the APIC brummagem project or a knowledgeable collector.

Repins

In searching for old campaign buttons, collectors have discovered caches of old button papers which were printed but never made into buttons. Some of those collectors thought the papers would be worth more if made into buttons. Buttons made long after an election, from original papers are called repins, and are in the same category as fakes and reproductions.

One way to easily tell a repin is to look at the metal on the back. If the button design is from the 1930s, 40s or 50s and the metal is painted white on the back, it is a repin. This is known because white-backed metal was not used on any buttons until the 1960s. The source of this metal is venetian blinds. Of course if the button is from a 1960s campaign white metal on the back does not mean that it is a fake. Not all repins have white metal backs, but the backs of repins are usually different from the originals. Again you should consult the APIC brummagem project, or compare the button to one known to be made in that year.

Another way to tell a repin is the surface of the button. Modern materials do not have the same look or feel of those from the 1940s. However, you must be familiar with both types of buttons to be sure.

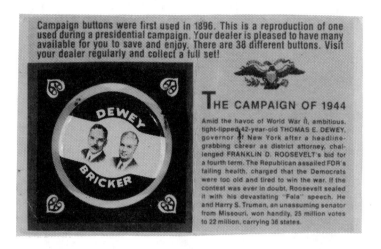

Campaign buttons were first used in 1896. This is a reproduction of one used during a presidential campaign. Your dealer is pleased to have many available for you to save and enjoy. There are 38 different buttons. Visit your dealer regularly and collect a full set!

THE CAMPAIGN OF 1944

Amid the havoc of World War II, ambitious, tight-lipped 42-year-old THOMAS E. DEWEY, governor of New York after a headline-grabbing career as district attorney, challenged FRANKLIN D. ROOSEVELT's bid for a fourth term. The Republican assailed FDR's failing health, charged that the Democrats were too old and tired to win the war. If the contest was ever in doubt, Roosevelt sealed it with his devastating "Fala" speech. He and Harry S. Truman, an unassuming senator from Missouri, won handily, 25 million votes to 22 million, carrying 36 states.

American Oil Co. reproduction on the original give-away card. No collector value.

Union bugs

   Some people believe that if a button has a "union bug" it is genuine, but such marking has nothing to do with the legitimacy of an item. A union bug is a marking on a printed item which indicates that it was manufactured with union labor. Candidates who seek the votes of union members feel it is important to have a union bug on their campaign materials. However today there are fewer unionized printers and much campaign material is being produced without union bugs.

120% $5-$10

   The button pictured is interesting. It has what appears to be a large union bug directly on its face (which is unusual, as they are normally hidden on the edge) but it is actually just hatchwork in the shape of a union bug.

Collecting for Fun or Profit

While many claim to enjoy their collecting hobby merely for the enjoyment the items bring, most people who are drawn to collecting things enjoy the fact that their acquisitions tend to rise in value.

Recent comments in collectible publications indicate that the reason for the rise in popularity of baseball cards over coins was the excitement of the possibility of receiving a rare card in a pack. It may be part of the new lottery craze, or perhaps collectors are all misers at heart, but the possibility of quick or steady profit excites most collectors.

One happy fact about collecting political items is that if you overpay for an item, it will usually reach that level sooner or later, usually during the next election. Every four years the hobby gets a new boost of excitement and new members as the presidential election gets under way.

In any case, collecting political items offers excellent investment opportunities as well as the pleasure derived from the historical significance of the items.

For those who do not wish to spend significant money on the hobby but enjoy studying the political issues of the times, there are numerous items available at minuscule prices. Items such as brochures, photographs, bumper stickers, jewelry and buttons for most candidates are available for less than a dollar or up to a couple dollars. For nearly every candidate there is some item available at a reasonable price.

For those who appreciate a rise in the value of their collection, political campaign items will fill the need. The values have risen steadily over the years. In the stamp collecting hobby, a stamp of which only 100 are available sells for over $100,000 and a unique item sells for nearly a million dollars. But in political collecting, unique items can be found for less than $10,000 and the highest price ever paid for a button was $50,000.

As with most collectibles, the best way to make a profit is to buy the rarest items in the best condition available. These usually lead the way in price appreciation. At the other end, cheap items in poor condition usually do not rise much in value. For example, a small, ugly Cox metal rooster stud sold for about $10 twenty years ago and today sells for $20 to $30. A large, colorful Cox fob which sold for $125 at the same time, now is worth $3,000 to $6,000.

If you can't afford the very best the next best choice is to collect what is popular. Colorful celluloid buttons are the most popular political item today and as more collectors begin collections there will be greater demand for them. Popular figures such as John F. Kennedy and Teddy Roosevelt attract many collectors. However, fads fade and what is popular today may not be popular a few years from now.

Another strategy is to try to anticipate demand. If you bought beautiful, colorful old buttons in the 1970s you would have seen them rise dramatically in value in the late 1980s. Many buttons priced at $25 to $75 in those days rose to several hundred or over a thousand dollars. If you start collecting inexpensive items today which become popular years from now, your retirement will be assured. Of course you can't count on clairvoyance, so you should be sure that you are collecting something you enjoy, regardless of its value. Many collectors specialize in a candidate they supported. For example, the campaigns of McCarthy, Reagan and Perot brought many collectors into the hobby.

Any of the recent presidents might be popular in years to come. While contemporary figures are considered flawed, their stature grows after their passing. Depending on your politics, Johnson, Nixon, Ford, Carter or Reagan might be good collections to start today. All of them have numerous items available in the 50¢ to $3 range, and all of them have enough items that it could take decades to come near completion. Of these, Ford is the most challenging, for while there are hundreds of varieties, only the most common are usually available. If you like underdogs, consider Humphrey, McGovern, Mondale or Dukakis. The rarest buttons of the twentieth century are the Democratic candidates who were trounced in 1920 and 1924. Will the buttons of their 1970s or '80s counterparts be the gems of the future?

Appendix 1: Resources

This appendix includes sources of further information for collectors of political items.

Organizations

There is only one organization for collectors of all types of political campaign items, the American Political Items Collectors. For $30 a year ($10 for youth) it offers a magazine three times a year, a subscription to the *Political Bandwagon* (a monthly newspaper, see below under periodicals), a roster listing all members in the country, many specialty chapters and regional and national conventions. Membership in APIC is the best way to improve your collection. For a membership application, send a self-addressed stamped business-size envelope to Mark Warda, P. O. Box 7, Clearwater, FL 34617. The APIC web site is located at:
> http://www.fred.net/ari/apic.html

Specialty Chapters

Within APIC thère are special chapters for people interested in the following types of items. By joining APIC you can also join the chapter(s) of your choice.

Carter	Kennedy	Franklin Roosevelt
Cause items	Labor history	Teddy Roosevelt
Clinton	Lincoln	Third parties/hopefuls
Democratic items	Local items	Truman
Ford	Reagan	Willkie
Goldwater		

Some of the chapters have their own listings on the following web page: http://www.fred.net/ari/apic.chapters.htm

Related Organizations

The following are a few organizations of collectors of items which may include political campaign items. If you collect political items in one of these specialties you may find these organizations a good source of material.

American Matchbook
    Collectors' Club
P. O. Box 18481
Ashville, NC 28814

Newspaper Collectors'
    Society of America
P. O. Box 19134
Lansing, MI 48901

American Philatelic Society
P. O. Box 8000
State College, PA

Nixon Collectors' Organization
975 Maunawili Cir.
Kailua, HI 96734-4620

Ephemera Society of America
P. O. Box 37
Schoharie, NY 12157

Paperweight Collectors' Assn.
P. O. Box1059
Easthampton, MA 01027-1059

National Sheet Music Society
1597 Fair Park Ave.
Los Angeles, CA 90041

Token and Medal Society
Cindy Grellman
P. O. Box 951988
Lake Mary, FL 32795

Books and Booklets

The most complete reference of political campaign items is a three volume set published by Ted Hake. The set was published over several years and the newer volumes include items missed in earlier volumes. Together the set covers over 12,000 different buttons. In 1991 an update was issued updating the values of the items. The three volumes are the following:
Encyclopedia of Political Buttons 1896-1972
Encyclopedia of Political Buttons Book II 1920-1976
Encyclopedia of Political Buttons III 1789-1916

For some candidates, collectors have cataloged the items into a single volume. If you plan to specialize in a single candidate these will be especially helpful.

John F. Kennedy:
The Campaign Buttons of John F. Kennedy
Bonnie Gardner & Harvey Goldberg
Self-published, 1980

J. F. K. Book II
Harvey Goldberg
Self-published, 1992

Robert F. Kennedy:
The Campaign Buttons of Robert F. Kennedy
Bonnie Gardner & Harvey Goldberg
Self-published, 1982

Richard M. Nixon:
The Political Collectibles of Richard Nixon
Eldon Almquist & Chris Crain
Self-published, 1989

Alton B. Parker:
Parker and Davis 1904
APIC, 1971

Adlai Stevenson:
Adlai E. Stevenson 1952-1956-1960
APIC, 1977

In addition to the above books, issues of the APIC *Keynoter* have been devoted to specific candidates and include much useful information. Back issues are available through the APIC.

Clinton	Winter, 1993	McCarthy, E.	Winter, 1989
Coolidge	Winter, 1992	McGovern	Winter, 1982
Davis	Fall/Winter, 1983	McKinley	Summer, 1984
Debs	Spring, 1991		*also*, Fall, 1984
Dewey	Spring, 1983	Rockefeller	Winter, 1990
Eisenhower	Winter, 1986	Roosevelt, F. D.	Spg./Sum., 1983
Goldwater	Summer, 1982	Roosevelt, T.	Summer, 1981
Hughes	Spring, 1988	Taft, W. H.	Spring, 1987
Johnson, L. B.	Spring, 1993	Truman	Summer, 1980
Kennedy, J. F.	Winter 1980	Willkie	Spring, 1986
Landon	Autumn, 1979	Wilson	Spring, 1982
Lodge, H. C., Jr.	Winter, 1991		

For collectors who specialize in a certain type of item, rather than a candidate, there are several guides available. Some of these are out of print but copies may be located through a determined search.

Badges and Medalets:
American Political Badges
and Medalets 1789-1892
Edmund B. Sullivan
Quarterman Publications, 1981

Cloth items:
Threads of History
Herbert Ridgeway Collins
Smithsonian Institution Press 1979

Canes:
Canes in the United States/
Illustrated Mementoes of
American History, 1607-1953
Catherine Dike
Cane Curiosa Press, 1994

Inaugural covers:
Noble's Catalog of Presidential
Inaugural Covers
Edward Krohn
Noble Publishing, 1990

Postcards:
Political Postcards 1900-1980
Bernard Greenhouse
Postcard Press, 1980

Tabs:
Political Tabs
Robert Warren
Robert Warren, 1991

Stamps:
Presidential Campaign Stamps
Mark Warda
Sphinx Publishing, 1990

Periodicals

The Political Bandwagon
P. O. Box 348
Leola, PA 17540

The Political Collector
P. O. Box 5171
York, PA 17405

Auctions

The following dealers regularly hold mail-bid auctions of political items. There is usually a charge of $3 to $10 for their catalogs, however, some may send you a free sample if you say you saw their address in this book.

Al Anderson
P. O. Box 644
Troy, OH 45373

The Political Gallery
5335 N. Tacoma Ave. #24
Indianapolis, IN 46220

David Frent
P. O. Box 455
Oakhurst, NJ 07755

Provenance
P. O. Box 3487
Wallington, NJ 07057

Hake's Americana
P. O. Box 1444
York, PA 17405

Rex Stark
49 Wethersfield Rd.
Bellington, MA 02019

HCA
3 Neptune Rd.
Poughkeepsie, NY 12601

Jack Wilson
P. O. Box 49271
Austin, TX 78765

Historicana
P. O. Box 348
Leola, PA 17540

Dealers

The following dealers regularly or occasionally issue fixed price lists of political items for sale.

Be-In Buttons
PO Box 35593
Houston, TX 77235

Gil Gleason
8 Altamount Dr.
Orinda, CA 94563

Mort Berkowitz
1501 Broadway #1808
New York, NY 10036

LBJ Museum
2313 Red River
Austin, TX 78705

Mark Evans
393 Genesee
Avon, NY 14414

Political Americana
1456 G Street NW
Washington, DC 20005

Tom French
P. O. Box 65360
Tucson, AZ 85728

Mark Warda
P. O. Box 7
Clearwater, FL 34617

The following world wide web sites feature political items:
http://www.political.com/buttons.html
http://www.permanentpromotions.com
http://www.polamericana.com/

Museums

Several museums have displays of political collectibles which are quite impressive. The two best collections are at the following museums:

Museum of American
Political Life
University of Hartford
Hartford, CT

National Museum of
American History
Smithsonian Institution
Washington, DC

In addition, all of our recent presidents have presidential libraries and museums, and many of these have displays of campaign items. The locations of those for our recent presidents are:

Herbert Hoover, West Branch, IA
Franklin D. Roosevelt, Hyde Park, NY

Harry S. Truman, Independence, MO
Dwight D. Eisenhower, Abilene, KS
John F. Kennedy, Boston, MA
Lyndon B. Johnson, Austin, TX
Richard M. Nixon, Yorba Linda, CA
Gerald Ford, Ann Arbor, MI
Jimmy Carter, Atlanta, GA and Plains, GA
Ronald Reagan, Simi Valley, CA
George Bush, College Station, TX

Shops

The following shops specialize in political items:

Capitol Stamp & Coin Co. Inc.
1701 L Street NW
Washington, DC 20036

Celebrate America
Faneuil Hall market
Boston, MA 02109

Political Americana
Harbor Place/Pratt Street
Baltimore, MD

Political Americana
685 - 15th Street NW
Washington, DC

Political Americana
Union Station, West Hall
Washington, DC

Political Americana
3222 M Street, NW
Washington, DC

Presidential Coin & Antique Co.
6550-I Little River Tpk.
Alexandria, VA 22312

Appendix 2: Presidential Nominees

The following is a checklist of the presidential and vice-presidential candidates for all political parties since 1896. This list will help you determine what year a particular button is from and to which party the candidates belong. Five sources we checked for vote totals all gave different figures. We have used the highest total found in each case.

Party (electoral vote)	Candidates	Popular vote
1896		
❏Republican (271)	William McKinley—Garret A. Hobart	7,113,734
❏Dem./People's Pop.(176)	William J. Bryan—Arthur Sewall	6,511,495
❏Gold Democratic	John M. Palmer—Simon B. Buckner	135,456
❏Prohibition	Joshua Levering—Hale Johnson	132,007
❏Socialist Labor	Charles H. Matchett—Matthew Maguire	36,475
❏National Prohibition	Charles E. Bentley—James H. Southgate	19,363
❏Silver	William J. Bryan—Arthur Sewall	
1900		
❏Republican (292)	William McKinley—Theodore Roosevelt	7,219,828
❏Democratic (155)	William J. Bryan—Adlai E. Stevenson	6,358,345
❏Prohibition	John G. Woolley—Henry B. Metcalf	210,200
❏Social Dem. Of America	Eugene V. Debs—Job Harriman	95,744
❏Populist	Wharton Barker—Ignatious Donnelly	50,605
❏Socialist-Labor	Joseph F. Malloney—Valentine Remmel	40,900
❏Union Reform	Seth H. Ellis—Samuel Nicholson	5,698
❏United Christian	Jonah F. R. Leonard—David H. Martin	5,500
❏National	Donelson Caffery—Archibald M. Howe	
❏People's/Fusionists	William J. Bryan—Adlai E. Stevenson	
❏Silver Republican	William J. Bryan—Adlai E. Stevenson	
❏Social Dem.Of U.S.A.	Job Harriman—Maximilian S. Hayes	
1904		
❏Republican (336)	Theodore Roosevelt—Charles W. Fairbanks	7,628,831
❏Democratic (140)	Alton B. Parker—Henry G. Davis	5,084,898
❏Socialist/Socialist Dem.	Eugene V. Debs—Benjamin Hanford	402,714
❏Prohibition	Silas C. Swallow—George W. Carroll	259,163
❏Populist	Thomas E. Watson—Thomas H. Tibbles	117,183
❏Socialist Labor	Charles H. Corregan—William W. Cox	33,737
❏Continental	Austin Holcomb—A. King	1,000
❏National Liberal/Colored	George E. Taylor—W. C. Payne	

1908

❑Republican (321)	William H. Taft—James S. Sherman	7,678,908
❑Democratic (162)	William J. Bryan—John W. Kern	6,412,294
❑Socialist	Eugene V. Debs—Benjamin Hanford	420,793
❑Prohibition	Eugene W. Chafin—Aaron S. Watkins	253,840
❑Independence	Thomas L. Hisgen—John T. Graves	82,872
❑Populist	Thomas E. Watson—Samuel W. Williams	29,100
❑Socialist Labor	August Gillhaus—Donald L. Munro	14,021
❑United Christian	Daniel B. Turner—Lorenzo S. Coffin	500

1912

❑Democratic (435)	T. Woodrow Wilson—Thomas R. Marshall	6,296,547
❑Progressive/Bull Moose (88)	Theodore Roosevelt—Hiram W. Johnson	4,119,538
❑Republican (8)	William H. Taft—James S. Sherman	3,486,720
❑Socialist	Eugene V. Debs—Emil Seidel	901,873
❑Prohibition	Eugene W. Chafin—Aaron S. Watkins	207,972
❑Socialist Labor	Arthur E. Reimer—August Gillhaus	29,374

1916

❑Democratic (277)	T. Woodrow Wilson—Thomas R. Marshall	9,129,606
❑Republican (254)	Charles E. Hughes—Charles W. Fairbanks	8,546,789
❑Socialist	Allan L. Benson—George R. Kirkpatrick	590,322
❑Prohibition	J. Frank Hanly—Ira Landrith	221,030
❑Progressive	Theodore Roosevelt—John M. Parker	35,054
❑Socialist Labor	Arthur E. Reimer—Caleb Harrison	15,284
❑American	William Sulzer—I.G. Pollard	

1920

❑Republican (404)	Warren G. Harding—Calvin Coolidge	16,153,115
❑Democratic (127)	James M. Cox—Franklin D. Roosevelt	9,147,353
❑Socialist	Eugene V. Debs—Seymour Stedman	919,799
❑Farmer Labor	Parley P. Christensen—Maximilian S. Hayes	265,411
❑Prohibition	Aaron S. Watkins—David L. Colvin	189,408
❑American	James E. Ferguson	48,000
❑Socialist Labor	William W. Cox—August Gillhaus	31,715
❑Single Tax	Robert C. Macauley—Richard C. Barnum	5,837

1924

❑Republican (382)	J. Calvin Coolidge—Charles G. Dawes	15,725,016
❑Democratic (136)	John W. Davis—Charles W. Bryan	8,386,704
❑Progressive/Socialist (13)	Robert M. La Follette—Burton K. Wheeler	4,832,532
❑Prohibition	Herman P. Faris—Marie C. Brehm	57,551
❑Socialist Labor	Frank T. Johns—Verne L. Reynolds	38,958
❑Communist/Workers	William Z. Foster—Benjamin Gitlow	36,386

❏American	Gilbert O. Nations—Charles H. Randall	24,340
❏Commonwealth Land	William J. Wallace—John C. Lincoln	2,948
❏Farmer Labor	William Z. Foster—Benjamin Gitlow	
❏National Independent	John Zahnd—Roy M. Harrop	
❏People's Progressive	Robert R. Pointer—Roy M. Harrop	

1928

❏Republican (444)	Hebert C. Hoover—Charles Curtis	21,437,277
❏Democratic (87)	Alfred E. Smith- Joseph T. Robinson	15,016,443
❏Socialist	Norman M. Thomas—James H. Maurer	267,835
❏Communist/Workers	William Z. Foster—Benjamin Gitlow	48,770
❏Socialist Labor	Verne L. Reynolds—Jeremiah D. Crowley	21,603
❏Prohibition	William F. Varney—James A. Edgerton	20,106
❏Farmer Labor	Frank E. Webb—LeRoy Tillman	6,390
❏National Independent	John Zahnd—Wesley H. Bennington	6,390
❏National Progressive	Dr. Henry Hoffman—Jane Addams	

1932

❏Democratic (472)	Franklin D. Roosevelt—James N. Garner	22,829,501
❏Republican (59)	Herbert C. Hoover—Charles Curtis	15,761,841
❏Socialist	Norman M. Thomas—John H. Maurer	884,781
❏Communist/Workers	William Z. Foster—James W. Ford	103,253
❏Prohibition	William D. Upshaw—Frank S. Regan	81,872
❏Liberty	William H. Harvey—Frank B. Hemenway	53,425
❏Socialist Labor	Verne L. Reynolds—John W. Aiken	34,043
❏Farmer Labor	Jacob S. Coxey—Julius J. Reiter	7,431
❏National Independent	John Zahnd—Florence Garvin	1,645
❏Jobless/Blue Shirts	James R. Cox—Victor C. Tisdal	740
❏Liberty And Unity	Frank E. Webb—Andrae Nordskog	

1936

❏Democratic (523)	Franklin D. Roosevelt—John N. Garner	27,757,333
❏Republican (8)	Alfred M. Landon—Frank Knox	16,684,231
❏Union	William Lemke—Thomas C. O'Brien	892,267
❏Socialist	Norman M. Thomas—George A. Nelson	187,833
❏Communist	Earl R. Browder—James W. Ford	80,171
❏Prohibition	D. Leigh Colvin—Claude A. Watson	37,847
❏Socialist Labor	John W. Aiken—Emil F. Teichert	12,829
❏Greenback	John Zahnd—Florence Garvin	
❏Christian	William D. Pelley	1,598

1940

❏Demoratic (449)	Fanklin D. Roosevelt—Henry A. Wallace	27,313,041
❏Republican (82)	Wendell L. Willkie—Charles L. McNary	22,348,480
❏Socialist	Norman M. Thomas—Maynard C. Krueger	116,410
❏Prohibition	Roger W. Babson—Edgar V. Moorman	58,708
❏Communist	Earl R. Browder—James W. Ford	46,251
❏Socialist Labor	John W. Aiken—Aaron M. Orange	14,892
❏Independent	Alfred Knutson	545
❏Greenback	John Zahnd—James E. Yates	

1944

❏Democratic (432)	Franklin D. Roosevelt—Harry S. Truman	25,612,610
❏Republican (99)	Thomas E. Dewey—John W. Bricker	22,017,617
❏Socialist	Norman M. Thomas—Darlington Hoopes	80,518
❏Prohibition	Claude A. Watson—Andrew Johnson	74,779
❏Socialist Labor	Edward A. Teichert—Arla A. Albaugh	45,336
❏America First	Gerald L. K. Smith—Harry A. Romer	1,780
❏Greenback ·	Leo C. Donnelly—Frank Jeffries	
❏Texas Regulars		135,444

1948

❏Democratic/Liberal (304)	Harry S. Truman—Alben W. Barkley	24,179,345
❏Republican (189)	Thomas E. Dewey—Earl Warren	21,991,291
❏States' Rts. (Dixiecrats) (38)	J. Strom Thurmond—Fielding L. Wright	1,176,125
❏Progressive	Henry A. Wallace—Glen H. Taylor	1,157,326
❏Socialist	Norman M. Thomas—Tucker P. Smith	139,572
❏Prohibition	Claude A. Watson—Dale H. Learn	103,900
❏Socialist Labor	Edward A. Teichert—Stephen Emery	29,272
❏Socialist Workers	Farrell Dobbs—Grace Carlson	13,613
❏Christian Nationalist	Gerald L. K. Smith—Harry A. Romer	42
❏Greenback	John G. Scott—Granville B. Leeke	6
❏American Vegetarian	John Maxwell—Symon Gould	4
❏Communist	Henry A. Wallace—Glen H. Taylor	

1952

❏Republican (442)	Dwight D. Eisenhower—Richard M. Nixon	33,936,252
❏Democratic (89)	Adlai E. Stevenson—John J. Sparkman	27,314,992
❏Progressive/American Labor	Vincent W. Hallinan—Charlotta A. Bass	140,138
❏Prohibition	Stuart Hamblen—Enoch A. Holtwick	72,949
❏Socialist Labor	Eric Hass—Stephen Emery	30,376
❏Socialist	Darlington Hoopes—Samuel H. Friedman	20,203
❏Constitution	Douglas A. MacArthur—Jack B. Tenny	17,205
❏Socialist Workers	Farrell Dobbs—Myra T. Weiss	10,312
❏Poor Man's Party	Henry J. Krajewski—Frank Jenkins	4,203

❑Constitution	Douglas A. MacArthur—Harry F. Byrd	2,911
❑America First	Douglas A. MacArthur—Harry F. Byrd	233
❑Constitution Of California	Douglas A. MacArthur—Vivien Kellems	178
❑American Vegetarian	Daniel J. Murphy—Symon Gould	
❑Greenback	Frederick C. Proehl—J. Edward Bedell	
❑Communist	Vincent W. Hallinan—Charlotta A. Bass	
❑Theocratic/Church Of God	Homer A. Tomlinson—Willie I. Bass	
❑Washington Peace	Ellen L. Jensen	

1956

❑Republican (457)	Dwight D. Eisenhower—Richard M. Nixon	35,590,472
❑Democratic/Liberal (74)	Adlai E. Stevenson—Estes Kefauver	26,028,887
❑Independent	T. Coleman Andrews—Thomas H. Werdel	275,915
❑States' Rights—Kentucky	Harry F. Byrd—William E. Jenner	134,157
❑Soc. Labor/Indust. Govt.	Eric Hass—Georgia Cozzini	44,450
❑Prohibition	Enoch A. Holtwick—Edwin M. Cooper	41,937
❑Texas Constitution	William E. Jenner—J. Bracken Lee	30,999
❑Socialist Workers	Farrell Dobbs—Myra T. Weiss	8,148
❑Black & Tan Grand Old Party	Dwight D. Eisenhower—Richard M. Nixon	4,313
❑Socialist	Darlington Hoopes—Samuel H. Friedman	2,192
❑American Third Party	Henry B. Krajewski—Anna M. Yezo	1,892
❑Christian Nationalist	Gerald L. K. Smith—Charles F. Robertson	8
❑Constitution	T. Coleman Andrews—Thomas H. Werdel	
❑States' Rights	Harry F. Byrd—Thomas H. Werdel	
❑American Vegetarian	Herbert M. Shelton—Symon Gould	
❑Greenback	Frederick C. Proehl—Edward K. Meador	
❑Pioneer	William Langer—Burr McCloskey	
❑South Carolinians for Independent Electors	Harry F. Byrd	

1960

❑Democratic (330)	John F. Kennedy—Lyndon B. Johnson	34,227,096
❑Republican (223)	Richard M. Nixon—Henry Cabot Lodge	34,108,647
❑Independent (15)	Harry F. Byrd	462,575
❑National States' Rights	Orval E. Faubus—John G. Crommelin	214,549
❑Soc. Labor/Industrial Govt.	Eric Hass—George Cozzini	47,522
❑Prohibition	Rutherford L. Decker—E. Harold Munn	46,220
❑Socialist Workers	Farrell Dobbs—Myra T. Weiss	40,175
❑Constitution of Texas	Charles L. Sullivan—Merritt B. Curtis	18,169
❑Conserv. of New Jersey	J. Bracken Lee—Kent H. Courtney	8,708
❑Virginia Conservative	C. Benton Coiner—Edward J. Silverman	4,204
❑Tax Cut	Lar (Lawrence J.S.) Daly—Bryan M. Miller	1,767
❑Ind. Afro-American Unity	Clennon King—Reginald Carter	1,485
❑Constitution	Merritt B. Curtis—Bryan M. Miller	1,401
❑Liberal	John F. Kennedy—Lyndon B. Johnson	

❏American Third	Henry B. Krajewski	
❏American Vegetarian	Symon Gould—Christopher Gian-Cursio	
❏Greenback	Whitney H. Slocomb—Edward K. Meador	
❏Mankind's Assembly	Lewis Bertrand	
❏Outer Space	Gabriel Green—Addison Brown	
❏Rocking Chair	Connie Watts—Ralph Raper	
❏Theocratic/Church Of God	Homer A. Tomlinson—Raymond L. Teague	
❏Independent	Jack Moore	
❏Independent	William L. Smith	
❏Independent	Agnes Waters	

1964

❏Democratic (486)	Lyndon B. Johnson—Hubert H. Humphrey	43,129,566
❏Republican (82)	Barry M. Goldwater—William Miller	27,178,188
❏Liberal	Lyndon Johnson—Hubert H. Humphrey	342,432
❏Alabama Unpledged Elec.		210,732
❏Socialist Labor	Eric Hass—Henning Blomen	45,219
❏Socialist Workers	Clifton DeBerry—Edward Shaw	32,720
❏Prohibition	E. Harold Munn—Mark Shaw	23,267
❏National States' Rights	John Kasper—J. B. Stoner	6,953
❏Constitution	Joseph B. Lightburn—Theodore Billings	5,090
❏Theocratic	Homer A. Tomlinson—William Rogers	20
❏Universal Party	James Hensley—John Hopkins	19
❏Peace	Mirhan Ask	10
❏America First	Lar (Lawrence J.S.) Daly	8
❏Car And Driver	Dan Gurney	6
❏Independent States' Rights	T. Coleman Andrews	
❏Best Party	Yette Bronstein	
❏American	Louis E. Jaeckel	
❏American Nazi	George L. Rockwell	
❏Metropolitan	Wilbur Huckle—Marv Throneberry	
❏National Tax Savers	D. X. B. Schwartz	
❏Poor Man's	Henry B. Krajewski—Ann Yezo	
❏United	Grant Van Tilborg—Harold Putnam	
❏United Nations	Emil Matalik	
❏Vegetarian	Symon Gould—Abram Wolfson	

1968

❏Republican (301)	Richard M. Nixon—Spiro Agnew	31,785,480
❏Democratic (191)	Hubert H. Humphrey—Edmund Muskie	31,275,166
❏American Independent (46)	George C. Wallace—Curtis LeMay	9,906,473
❏Liberal	Hubert H. Humphrey—Edmund Muskie	311,622
❏Socialist Labor	Henning A. Blomen—George Taylor	52,594
❏Freedom And Peace	Dick Gregory—D. Frost, M. Lane, B. Spock	47,133

❑Socialist Workers	Fred Halstead—Paul Boutelle	41,389
❑Peace And Freedom	Eldridge Cleaver—(various)	36,565
❑New Party	Eugene J. McCarthy—John Lindsey	27,067
❑Prohibition	E. Harold Munn—Rolland Fisher	15,123
❑People's Constitutional	Ventura Chavez—Adelicio Moya	1,519
❑Communist	Charlene Mitchell—Michael Zagarell	1,075
❑Universal	James Hensley—Roscoe MacKenna	142
❑Constitution	Richard K. Troxell—Merl Thayer	34
❑Berkley Defense Group	Kent M. Soeters—James Powers	17
❑America First	Lar (Lawrence J.S.) Daly	
❑Theocratic	Homer A. Tomlinson—W. B.McKenzie	

1972

❑Republican (520)	Richard M. Nixon—Spiro Agnew	47,169,911
❑Democratic (17)	George S. McGovern—Sargent Shriver	29,170,383
❑American	John G. Schmitz—Thomas Anderson	1,107,083
❑Liberal	George McGovern—Sargent Shriver	183,128
❑Socialist Workers	Linda Jenness—Andrew Pulley	97,295
❑People's	Benjamin Spock—Julius Hobson	78,889
❑Socialist Labor	Louis Fisher—Genevieve Gunderson	53,815
❑Communist	Gus Hall—Jarvis Tyner	25,621
❑Socialist Workers	Evelyn Reed	13,878
❑Prohibition	E. Harold Munn—Marshall Uncapher	13,505
❑Libertarian (1)	John Hospers—Theodora Nathan	3,697
❑America First	John V. Mahalchik—Irving Homer	1,743
❑Independent	Edward Wallace—Robert Mess	460
❑Universal	˙Gabriel Green—Daniel Fry	220

1976

❑Democratic (297)	James E. Carter—Walter Mondale	40,830,763
❑Republican (241)	Gerald R. Ford—Robert Dole	39,147,793
❑Independent	Eugene J. McCarthy	756,691
❑Libertarian	Roger MacBride—David Bergland	173,011
❑American Independent	Lester G. Maddox—William Dyke	170,780
❑American	Thomas J. Anderson—Rufus Shackleford	160,773
❑Socialist Workers	Peter Camejo—Willie Mae Reid	91,314
❑Communist	Gus Hall—Jarvis Tyner	59,114
❑People's Party	Margaret Wright—Benjamin Spock	49,024
❑U.S. Labor	Lyndon H. LaRouche Jr.—R. W. Evans	40,045
❑Prohibition	Benjamin C. Bubar—Earl Dodge	15,934
❑Socialist Labor	Jules Levin—Constance Blomen	9,616
❑Socialist	Frank P. Zeidler—J. Quinn Brisben	6,038
❑Restoration	Ernest L. Miller—Roy Eddy	361
❑United American	Frank Taylor—Henry Swan	36

❑Constitutional	Paul Cunningham	
❑Independent	Billy Joe Clegg—Auburn L. Packwood	
❑Independent	F. D. Kirkpatrick	
❑Independent	Donald Jackson	
❑Independent	Kenyon Knourek	
❑Independent	Ellen McCormack	
❑Independent	Pat Patton	
❑Independent	Chief Burning Wood—Austin Burton	

1980

❑Republican (489)	Ronald W. Reagan—George H. W. Bush	43,904,153
❑Democratic (49)	James E. Carter—Walter Mondale	35,483,883
❑National Unity Campaign	John B. Anderson—Patrick Lucey	5,720,060
❑Libertarian	Edward Clark—David Koch	921,299
❑Citizens	Barry Commoner—Ladonna Harris	234,294
❑Communist	Gus Hall—Angela Davis	45,954
❑American Independent	John R. Rarick—Eileen Shearer	41,268
❑Socialist Workers	Clifton DeBerry—Matilde Zimmerman	40,145
❑Right To Life	Ellen McCormack—Carroll Driscoll	32,327
❑Peace And Freedom	Maureen Smith—Elizabeth Barron	18,117
❑Workers World	Deirdre Griswold—Larry Holmes	13,300
❑Statesman	Benjamin C. Bubar—Earl Dodge	7,212
❑Socialist	David McReynolds-Diane Drufenbrock	6,898
❑American	Percy L. Greaves—Frank Varnum	6,647
❑Socialist Workers	Andrew Pulley—Matilde Zimmerman	6,272
❑Socialist Workers	Richard Congress-Matilde Zimmerman	4,029
❑Middle Class	Kurt Lynen—Harry Kieve	3,694
❑Down With Lawyers	Bill Gahres—J. F. Loghlin	1,718
❑American	Frank W. Shelton—George Jackson	1,555
❑Independent	Martin E. Wendelken	923
❑Natural Peoples League	Harley McLain—Jewelie Goeller	296
❑Independent	Luther Wilson	
Write-Ins		16,921

1984

❑Republican (525)	Ronald W. Reagan—George H. W. Bush	54,455,075
❑Democratic (13)	Walter F. Mondale—Geraldine Ferraro	37,577,185
❑Libertarian	David Bergland—Jim Lewis	228,314
❑Independent	Lyndon H. LaRouche Jr.—Billy Davis	78,807
❑Citizens	Sonia Johnson—Richard Walton	72,200
❑Populist	Bob Richards—Maureen Kennedy Salaman	66,336
❑Independent Alliance	Dennis L. Serrette—Nancy Ross	46,868
❑Communist	Gus Hall— Angela Davis	36,386
❑Socialist Workers	Mel Mason—Andrea Gonzalez	24,706

❑Workers World	Larry Holmes—Gloria Lariva	15,329
❑American	Delmar Davis—Traves Brownlee	13,161
❑Workers League	Ed Winn—E. Berganzi, J. Brust, H. Halyard	10,801
❑Prohibition	Earl F. Dodge—Warren C. Martin	4,242
❑Workers World	Gabrielle Holmes—Milton Vera	2,656
❑Nat. Unity Party of Ky.	John B. Anderson	1,486
❑Big Deal	Gerald Baker	892
❑United Sovereign Citizens	Arthur J. Lowery	825
❑Independent	Neil K. Filoa	
❑Independent	William J. Dupont	

1988

❑Republican (426)	George H. Bush—Dan Quayle	48,886,097
❑Democratic (111)	Michael S. Dukakis—Lloyd Bentsen	41,809,074
❑Libertarian	Ron Paul—Andre V. Marrou	432,179
❑New Alliance	Lenora B. Fulani—Joyce Dattner (and others)	217,219
❑Populist	David E. Duke—Floyd Parker	47,047
❑Consumer	Eugene J. McCarthy—Florence Rice	30,905
❑American Independent	James C. Griffin—Charles "Chuck" Morsa	27,818
❑Natl. Economic Recovery	Lyndon H. LaRouche Jr.	25,562
❑Right to Life	William A. Marra—John Andrews	20,504
❑Workers League	Ed Winn—Barry Porster	18,693
❑Socialist Workers	James Warren—Kathleen Mickells	15,604
❑Peace and Freedom	Herbert Lewis—Emma Mar	10,370
❑Prohibition	Earl F. Dodge—George Ormsby	8,002
❑Workers World	Larry Holmes—Gloria LaRiva	7,846
❑Socialist	Willa Kenoyer—Ron Ehrenreich	3,882
❑American	Delmar Dennis—Earl Jeppson	3,476
❑Grassroots	Jack E. Herer	1,949
❑Independent	Louie G. Youngkeit	372
❑Third World Assembly	John G. Martin	236
❑Independent	Neil K. Filoa	
❑Independent	Jack Moore	

1992

❑Democratic (370)	William J. Clinton—Albert Gore Jr.	44,909,326
❑Republican (168)	George H. Bush—Dan Quayle	38,117,331
❑Independent	Ross Perot—James Stockdale	19,714,657
❑Libertarian	Andre V. Marrou—Nancy Lord	291,627
❑Populist	James " Bo" Gritz—Cy Minette	107,014
❑New Alliance	Lenora B. Fulani—Elizabeth Munz	73,714
❑U. S. Taxpayers	Howard Phillips—Gen. Aldion Knight	43,434
❑Natural Law	John Hagelin—Dr. Mike Tompkins	39,179
❑Peace & Freedom	Ron Daniels—Asiba Tupahache	27,961

❏Economic Recovery	Lyndon H. LaRouche Jr.—James Bevel (and others)	26,333
❏Socialist Workers	James Warren—Estelle DeDate	23,096
❏Independent	Drew Bradford	4,749
❏Grassroots	Jack E. Herer—Derrick P. Grimmer	3,875
❏Socialist	J. Quinn Brisben—William D. Edwards*	3,057
❏Workers League	Helen Halyard—Fred Mazelis	3,050
❏Take Back America	John Yiamouyiannas—Allen C. McCone	2,199
❏Independent	Delbert L. Ehlers—Rick Wendt	1,149
❏Prohibition	Earl F. Dodge—George Ormsby	961
❏Apathy	Jim Boren—Bill Wiedman	956
❏Third	Eugene A. Hem—JoanneRolland	405
❏Looking Back	Isabell Masters—Walter Masters	339
❏American	Robert J. Smith—Doris Feimer	292
❏Workers World	Gloria LaRiva—Larry Holmes	181
❏Queer Nation	Terence Smith—Joan Jett Blakk	

*Edwards died prior to the election and was replaced by Barbara Garson

Appendix 3: Presidential Hopefuls

The following is a list of persons who have sought, or have had the support of others for, their nomination for president.

1896 Hopefuls

Republicans
William Allison
Cornelius Bliss
William Bradley
James Cameron
Hamilton Fish, Jr.
Benjamin Harrison
William Linton
Levi Morton
Matthew Quay
Thomas Reed.

$40-$60

Democrats
John Charles Black
Joseph Blackburn
Richard Bland
Horace Boies
James Campbell
Grover Cleveland
David Hill
Claude Matthews
John McLean
William Morrison
Robert Pattison
Sylvestor Pennoyer
William Russell
Adlai Stevenson
Henry Teller
Benjamin Tillman
David Turpie

$25-$40

1900

Republicans
George Dewey

1904 Hopefuls

Republicans
John Hay
Marcus Hanna
Cyrus Waldbridge

$50-$75

Democrats
Francis Cockrell
Bird Coler
Arthur Gorman
George Gray
Judson Harmon
William Randolph Hearst
Tom Johnson
George McClellan
Nelson Miles
Richard Olney
Robert Pattison
Charles Towne
Edward Wall
John Williams

$20-$40

1908 Hopefuls

Republicans
Joseph G. Cannon
George Courtelyou
Charles Fairbanks
Joseph Foraker
Charles Evans Hughes
Philander Knox
Robert LaFollette
Theodore Roosevelt
William Warner

$25-$50

$60-$100

Democrats
Augustus Bacon
Lewis Stuyvesant Chanler
Charles Culberson
Edgar Cullen
John Daniel
John Joseph Douglass
Joseph W. Folk
Melville W. Fuller
William Gaynor
George Gray
Judson Harmon
John Johnson
Tom Johnson
Rufus Peckham
Edward White
John Williams
Woodrow Wilson

$30-$50

1912 Hopefuls

Democrats
Simeon Baldwin
William Jennings Bryan
John Burke
James Beauchamp "Champ" Clark
Eugene Foss
William Gaynor
Judson Harmon
Ollie James
John Kern
James Lewis
Thomas Marshall
William Sulzer
Oscar Underwood

Republicans
Albert Beveridge
Albert Cummins
Herbert Hadley
Charles Evans Hughes
Robert LaFollette
Theodore Roosevelt

$50-$80

$40-$60

$20-$30

1916 Hopefuls

Republicans
Edward Babcock
William Borah
Martin Brumbaugh
Theodore Burton
Albert Cummins
Thomas du Pont
Charles Fairbanks
Henry Ford
Warren G. Harding
Philander Knox
Robert LaFollette

$3-$8

More Republicans
Henry Cabot Lodge
James Robert Mann
Samuel McCall
Theodore Roosevelt
Elihu Root
Lawrence Y. Sherman
William Howard Taft
John Wanamaker
John W. Weeks
Charles Whitman
Frank Willis
Leonard Wood

1920 Hopefuls

Republicans
William Borah
Nicholas Murray Butler
Calvin Coolidge
Thomas du Pont
M. C. Gregor
Jacob Harmon
William Hayes
Herbert Hoover
Hiram Johnson
Frank Kellogg
Philander Knox
Robert LaFollette
Irvine Lenroot
Frank Lowden
Samuel Nauclain
Gen. John Pershing
Miles Poindexter
Jeter Pritchard
William Sproul
George Sutherland
Howard Sutherland
Charles Warren
Francis Warren
James Watson
Leonard Wood

$20-$30

$20-$30

Democrats
Newton Baker
Charles W. Bryan
William Jennings Bryan
James Beauchamp "Champ" Clark
Bainbridge Colby
Homer Cummings
Josephus Daniels
John W. Davis
Edward Edwards
James Gerard
Carter Glass
Francis Harrison
William Randolph Hearst
Gilbert Hitchcock
Ring Lardner
Thomas Marshall
William Gibbs McAdoo
Edwin Meredith
Robert Owen
A. Mitchell Palmer
Atlee Pomerone
Furnifold Simmons
Al Smith
Oscar Underwood
John Williams
Woodrow Wilson
Edward Wood

1924 Hopefuls

Republicans
Theodore Burton
Charles Chapman
Charles Dawes
James Harbord
Herbert Hoover
Wllliam Kenyon
Hiram Johnson
Robert LaFollette
Frank Lowden
James Watson

Democrats
Newton Baker
M. Behrman
Fred Brown
Royal Copeland
James Cox
Homer Cummings
Josephus Daniels
Jonathan Davis
William Dever

$35-$50

More Democrats
Woodbridge Ferris
Henry Ford
James Gerard
Carter Glass
Byron Harrison
David Houston
Cordell Hull
John Kendrick
Thomas R. Marshall
William Gibbs McAdoo
Edwin Meredith
Robert Owen
Samuel Ralston
Albert C. Ritchie
Joseph Robinson
Willard Saulsbury
George Silzer
Alfred E. Smith
William Sweet
Houston Thompson
Oscar Underwood
Thomas Walsh

$75-$150

1928 Hopefuls

Republicans
Calvin Coolidge
Charles Curtis
Charles Dawes
Alvan Fuller
Guy Goff
Charles Evans Hughes
Frank Lowden
George Norris
Robert Ross
James Watson
Frank Willis

Democrats
William Ayres
Theodore Bilbo
Victor Donahey
Walter George
Byron Harrison
Gilbert Hitchcock
Cordell Hull
Jesse Jones
Thomas W. McAdoo
Atlee Pomerene
James Reed
Houston Thompson
Richard Watts
Evans Woollen

$20-$30

1932 Hopefuls

Democrats
Newton Baker
H. O. Bentley
Harry Byrd
James Cox
Victor Donahey
John Nance Garner
William Randolph Hearst
James Hamilton Lewis
William McAdoo
William H. Murray
James Reed
Albert Ritchie
Joe Robinson
Will Rogers
Alfred E. Smith
Melvin Traylor
George White
Owen Young

Republicans
John Blaine
Calvin Coolidge
Jacob Coxey
Charles Dawes
Joseph France
Hiram Johnson
George S. Norris
James Wadsworth

$50-$75

1936 Hopefuls

Republicans
William Borah
Lester Dickinson
Walter Edge
Warren Green

$20-$30

Herbert Hoover
Frank Knox
Harry Nice
Robert Taft
Arthur Vandenberg
Earl Warren

$25-$35

1940 Hopefuls

Democrats
William Bankhead
Bennett "Champ" Clark
George Earle
James Farley
John Nance Garner
Cordell Hull
Paul McNutt
Frank Murphy
Ellis Patterson
Millard Tydings
Burton K. Wheeler

$15-$20

Republicans
Bruce Barton
Henry Styles Bridges
Harlan Bushfield
Arthur Capper
Thomas E. Dewey
Frank Gannett
Herbert Hoover
Arthur James
Fiorella LaGuardia
Hanford MacNider
Charles McNary
Joseph Martin
Robert Taft
Arthur Vandenberg

1944 Hopefuls

$5-$10

Democrats
Harry Byrd
James Farley
Fred Hildebrandt

Republicans
Riley Bender
John Bricker
Everett M. Dirksen
Douglas MacArthur
Robert McCormack
Harold Stassen
Earl Warren
Wendell Willkie

1948 Hopefuls

$40-$60

Democrats
William O. Douglas
Dwight D. Eisenhower
Leon Henderson
Herbert Holdridge
Ben Lanley
Scott Lucas
Paul McNutt
Joseph O'Mahoney
Claude Pepper
Richard Russell
Henry Wallace

Republicans
Raymond Baldwin
Riley Bender
Everett McKinley Dirksen
Alfred Driscoll
Dwight Green
Douglas MacArthur
Edward Martin
Joseph Martin Jr.
Brazilla Reece
Harold Stassen
Robert Taft
Arthur Vandenberg
Earl Warren

$25-$35

1952 Hopefuls

Republicans
Riley Bender
Alfred Driscoll
Douglas MacArthur
Wayne Morse
Harold Stassen
Robert Taft
Earl Warren
Thomas Werdel

$25-$50

Democrats
Alben Barkley
Edmund G. Brown
Robert Bulkley
Paul Dever
Paul H. Douglas
Wllliam O. Douglas
Oscar Ewing
James Fullbright
W. Averell Harriman
Hubert H. Humphrey
Estes Kefauver
Robert Kerr
Brien (Jason O'Brien) McMahon
James Murray
Claude Pepper
Sam Rayburn
Richard Russell
Harry Truman
G. Mennen Williams

1956 Hopefuls

Republicans
S. C. Arnold
John Bricker
John Foster Dulles
Christian Herter
William F. Knowland
Richard Nixon
Harold Stassen

Democrats
John Battle
Albert "Happy" Chandler
James Davis
William Averell Harriman
Lyndon B. Johnson
Walter Jones
Estes Kefauver
Frank Lausche
Warren Magnuson
John McCormack
Edmund S. Muskie
Stuart Symington
George Timmerman, Jr.

$2-$4

1960 Hopefuls

Democrats
Ross Barnett
Chester Bowles
Edmund G. "Pat' Brown
George Docking
Orval Faubus
Paul Fisher
Hubert H. Humphrey
Lyndon B. Johnson
Estes Kefauver
Herschel Loveless
Robert Meyner
Albert Rosellini
George Smathers
Adlai Stevenson
Stuart Symington

Republicans
Frank Beckwith
Edgar Eisenhower
Milton Eisenhower
Paul Fisher
Barry Goldwater
Walter Judd
Henry Cabot Lodge, Jr.
Nelson Rockefeller
Harold Stassen

$2-$4

$2-$4

1964 Hopefuls

Republicans
Hiram Fong
Walter Judd
Henry Cabot Lodge
Richard Nixon
Nelson Rockefeller
George Romney
William Scranton
Margaret Chase Smith

Democrats
Daniel Brewster
Hubert H. Humphrey
Robert F. Kennedy
Albert Porter
John Reynolds
Adlai E. Stevenson
George C. Wallace
Matthew Walsh

1968 Hopefuls

Republicans
Frank Carlson
Clifford Case
John Lindsay
Ronald Reagan
James Rhodes
Nelson Rockefeller
Winthrop Rockefeller
George Romney
Raymond Schafer
William Scranton
Harold Stassen
Strom Thurmond
John Tower
John Volpe

Democrats
James Fulbright
James Gray
Eugene McCarthy
Edward M. Kennedy
Robert F. Kennedy
Claude Kirk
George McGovern
Dan Moore
Pat Paulsen
Channing Phillips
George Smathers
Jesse Unruh
George C. Wallace
Stephen M. Young

$1-$3

$4-$8

1972 Hopefuls

Republicans
Paul McCloskey
John Ashbrook

$1-$3

Democrats
Shirley Chisolm
Ramsey Clark
Walter E. Fauntroy
Vance Hartke
Fred Harris
Wayne Hays
Harold Hughes
Hubert H. Humphrey
Henry Jackson
Edward M. Kennedy
John V. Lindsay
Eugene McCarthy
Wilbur Mills
Patsy Mink
Walter Mondale
Edmund Muskie
Terry Sanford
George C. Wallace
Sam Yorty

70% $3-$5

$3-$5

1976 Hopefuls

Democrats
Birch Bayh
Lloyd Bentsen
Jerry Brown
Robert Byrd
Frank Church
Fred Harris
Hubert H. Humphrey
Henry Jackson
Edward M. Kennedy
Edmund S. Muskie
George Roden
Ray Rollinson
Terry Sanford
Milton Shapp
Sargent Shriver
Morris Udall
George C. Wallace

Republicans
William Buckley
Neil K. Filoa
Charles Percy
Ronald Reagan

$1-$2

70% $4-$8

1980 Hopefuls

Republicans
John Anderson
Donald Badgley
Howard Baker
Nick Belluso
George Bush
William Carlson
Alvin Carris
John Connally
Phil Crane
Robert Dole
Ben Fernandez
Neil K. Filoa
Gerald Ford
V. A. Kelley
Jack Kemp
Harold Stassen
R. W. Yeager

Democrats
Frank Ahern
Jerry Brown
Cliff Finch
Richard Kay
Edward M. Kennedy
Lyndon LaRouche, Jr.
Scotty Larsen
Bob Maddox
Edmund S. Muskie
Don Reaux
Ray Rollinson
Daniel Sanderson

70% $2-$5

Note anti-Reagan slogan. $3-$5

1984 Hopefuls

Republicans
Gary Arnold
Ben Fernandez
David Kelley
Sandra Day O'Connor
Harold Stassen

Democrats
Reuben Askew
Bob Brewster
Alan Cranston
John Glenn
Robert Griser
Gary Hart
Ernest Hollings
Jesse Jackson
Richard Kay   70%
Stephen Koczak
Lyndon LaRouche, Jr.
George McGovern
Ray Rollinson
Alfred Timinski
Betty Jean Williams
Gerald Willis

$2-$5

$3-$6

1988 Hopefuls

Democrats
Bruce Babbitt
Joseph Biden
Bill Clinton
Mario Cuomo
Richard Gephardt
Albert Gore, Jr.
Gary Hart
Lee Iacocca
Jesse Jackson
Sam Nunn
Pat Paulsen
Ray Rollinson
Pat Schroeder
Paul Simon

Republicans
Robert Dole
Pierre "Pete" DuPont
Ben Fernandez
Alexander Haig
Jack Kemp
Jeane Kirkpatrick
Paul Laxalt
Pat Robertson

70% $2-$4

70% $3-$6

1992 Hopefuls

Democrats

Jerry Brown
Mario Cuomo
Tom Harkin
Bob Kerry
Eugene McCarthy
Ralph Nader
Pat Paulsen
Jay Rockefeller
Paul Tsongas
Doug Wilder

Republicans

Pat Buchanan

$3-$6

$3-$6

1996 Hopefuls

Republicans
Lamar Alexander
James Baker
William Bennett
Pat Buchanan
Dick Cheney
Charles Collins
Robert Dole
Robert K. Dornan
Malcolm S. (Steve) Forbes
Newt Gingrich
Phil Gramm
Jack Kemp
Alan Keyes
Rush Limbaugh
Colin Powell
Tom Shellenberg
Arlen Specter
Morry Taylor
Tommy Thompson
Pete Wilson

Democrats
Bruce Daniels
Jesse Jackson
Lyndon LaRouche
Pat Paulsen

$2-$3

$2-$3

$2-$3

Appendix 4: Political Initials & Acronyms

The following is a list of slogans and acronyms used on presidential campaign items in the last century which have obscure meanings. This list will help you determine if a button with an unusual slogan was from a presidential campaign.

ABC	Anybody but Carter (1980)
ABJ	Anybody but Johnson (1968)
ABK	Anybody but Kennedy (1968, 1980)
ACTWU	American Clothing and Textile Workers Union
ADA	Americans for Democratic Action
AFSCME	American Federation of State, County& Municipal Employees
AFGE	American Federation of Government Employees
AIP	American Independent Party
ALP	American Labor Party
BAM	Black American Movement (McCarthy 1968)
BGB	Barry Goldwater Backer (1964)
BMG	Barry M. Goldwater (1964)
BRAC	Brotherhood of Railway & Airline Clerks
CC	Calvin Coolidge (1924)
CDA	Coalition for a Democratic Alternative
CDC	California Democratic Council
$C_5H_4N_4O_3$	Formula for Urine ("$C_5H_4N_4O_3$ on AuH_2O" anti-Goldwater 1964)
CIC	Coalition for a Independant Candidacy (McCarthy 1968)
C.I.D.W.I.	Central Illinois Democratic Women, Inc.
C/M	Carter - Mondale (1976,1980)
COPE	Committee on Political Education
CPUSA	Communist Party of the U.S.A.
CTA/NEA	California Teachers Assn./National Education Assn.
CWA	Communications Workers of America
DFR	Defeat Franklin Roosevelt
DWG	Distillery Workers Guild
EMc2	Eugene McCarthy a 2nd time (1972)
EMK	Edward M. Kennedy
ESM	Edmund Sixtus Muskie
FBBI	For Bush Before Iowa (1980)
FCBNH	For Carter Before New Hampshire (1976)
FDP	Freedom Democratic Party
FDR	Franklin D. Roosevelt
FEF	Forget Eisenhower Forever (1956)
FKBW	For Kennedy Before Wisconsin (1960)

FMBDNC	For McGovern Before the Democratic National Convention
FMBM	For McGovern Before Miami
FMBNH	For McCarthy Before New Hampshire (1968)
FMBNH	For McGovern Before New Hampshire (1972)
F3C	Rule F(3)(c) requiring democratic delegates to vote for candidate they were elected for (1980)
G	Goldwater (1964)
GMG	George McGovern
GOP	Grand Old Party (Republican)
HHH	Hubert Horatio Humphrey (1968)
H3	Hubert Horatio Humphrey (1968)
IAK	I Adore Kennedy (1960)
IAM	International Association of Machinists
IDC/NDC	Illinois Democratic Coalition/National Democratic Coalition
IBEW	Internat'l Brotherhood of Electrical Workers
IB of TCS&H	International Brotherhood of Teamsters, Chauffers, Stablemen & Helpers
IGHAT	I'm Gonna Hate All Trumans *or* I'm Gonna Holler About Taxes (1948) *or* Ike's Gotta Have Another Term (1956)
ILA	International Longshoreman's Assn.
IT	Ike Twice (1956)
IUE	International Union of Electricians
IUOE	International Union of Operating Engineers
IVI	Independent Voters of Illinois
IWW	International Workers of the World
IYHYKHR	In Your Heart You Know He's Right (Goldwater 1964)
JC	Jimmy Carter (1976, 1980)
K7UGA in 64	Goldwater's CB license (1964)
K-J	Kennedy- Johnson (1960)
KMA	Kiss My Ass (McGovern 1972)
KNKC	Keep Nebraka Kennedy Conscious
La Tei YAaNi	Barry Goldwater's Name in Navajo (1964)
LNPL	Labor's Non- Partisan League
LOTE	Lesser of Two Evils (Carter 1980)
M Go Fritz	University of Michigan for Mondale (1984)
McG/25	McGovern/$25 donation (1972)
MEA /NEA	Minnesota Education Assn./Nat'l Education
N/A	Nixon & Agnew (1968, 1972)
NASW	National Association of Social Workers
NEA	National Education Association
NJEA/PAC	New Jersey Education Assn. / Political Action Committee
NOW	National Organization of Women
Oct.9th	Date Nixon gave a speech (McGovern 1972)
PAC	Political Action Committee

PFP	Peace & Freedom Party (1968)
PT 109	John F. Kennedy's WWII boat number (1960)
R&B	Reagan & Bush (1980, 1984)
RIF	Reduction in Force (anti-Reagan, 1984)
RIJ	Republicans & Independant for Johnson (1964)
RJ	Roosevelt & Johnson (1912)
RK is OK by JC	Robert Kennedy is okay by James Carter (1968)
R & R	Reagan & Rockefeller (1968)
RR	Ronald Reagan
SEIU	Service Employees Internationl Union
SIE	Society of Industrial Engineers
SIN	Stop Inflation Now
SLP	Socialist Labor Party
SOB Club	Save Our Business Club (anti-JFK)
TANSTAAFL	There Ain't No Such Thing as a Free Lunch (Hospers 1972)
TASK	Teen-Agers for Stevenson & Kefauver (1956)
TED 48	Thomas E. Dewey 1948
TGFMLU	Thank God for Mondale & Labor Unions
TIRCC	This Is Reagan Country Club
TMK	Too Many Kennedys (anti-EMK)
TRT	Taxpayers Revivalist Ticket
T.S.	Taft & Sherman
TTP	Tired Tax Payers
TUIT	To It as in "when I get around to it"
UWA-CIO	United Auto Workers-Congress of Industrial Organizations
UFCW	United Food & Commercial Workers
UFT	United Federation of Teachers
UFW	United Farm Workers
UMWA	United Mine Workers of America
UPWA-CIO	Union Printing Workers Association
URFI	United Republican Fund of Illinois
URW	United Rubber Workers
USWA	United Steel Workers of America
UYN	United Youth for Nixon (1968)
VFBG	Vote for Barry Goldwater (1964)
VIP	Voice in Politica (Wallace 1968)
VV	Vietnam Veterans (McCarthy 1968)
W&M	Wilson & Marshall (1912, 1916)
WCTU	Women's Christian Temperance Union
WIN	Whip Inflation Now (Ford, 1976)
YAF	Young Americans for Freedom
YAFK	Young Americans for Kennedy
YCERSOYA	You Can't Elect Republicans Sitting on Your Ass (1950s)
YD	Young Democrats

YP	Young Professionals
YPR	Young Professionals for Ronald Reagan
YRC	Young Republican Clubs
3G/B	George Bush (represents polls showing 3% support)
3H	Hubert Horatio Humphrey
8(Ball)	Behind the 8 ball (anti-FDR 1940, anti-Truman 1948)
16 to 1	Proposed silver to gold ratio (Bryan 1896, 1900)
26 million club	Goldwater's vote total (1964)
60 (on a "V")	Oregon button for Kennedy 1960
50,001	Oregon primary vote for Dewey
250, 000	Young Republicans supporting Nixon

Occasionally you might come across an items which merely says something like "Vote Democratic Nov. 8th." By looking at the chart below and the approximate age of the item you can determine which election it is from and therefore which candidate it supports. Keep in mind, though, that municipal and state elections are also held in years between presidential elections.

Nov. 2	Election day, 1920, 1948, 1976
Nov. 3	Election day, 1896, 1908, 1936, 1964, 1992
Nov. 4	Election day, 1924, 1952, 1980
Nov. 5	Election day, 1912, 1940, 1968, 1996
Nov. 6	Election day, 1900, 1928, 1956, 1984
Nov. 7	Election day, 1916, 1944, 1972, 2000
Nov. 8	Election day, 1904, 1932, 1960, 1988

Index